Roll of Honour 1939 – 1945 Swindon & District

KATHERINE COLE

Local Studies, Swindon Libraries

LOC02
2017

First published in the United Kingdom in 2017

© Local Studies (Swindon Libraries) 2017

Published for Local Studies (Swindon Libraries)
Central Library, Regent Circus, Swindon SN1 1QG
www.swindon.gov.uk/localstudies

by The Hobnob Press, Unit 30C, Deverill Road Trading Estate, Sutton Veny, Warminster BA12 7BZ

Katherine Cole has asserted her right under the Copyright, Designs and Patents Act 1988 to be identified as author of this work.

All rights reserved. No part of this publication may be reproduced, stored in a retrieval system, or transmitted in any form or by any means, electronic, mechanical, photocopying, recording or otherwise, without the prior permission of the publisher and copyright holder.

LOC02

British Library Cataloguing in Publication Data
A catalogue record for this book is available from the British Library

ISBN 978-1-906978-49-5

Typeset in Adobe Caslon Pro. Typesetting and origination by John Chandler

Printed by Lightning Source

Also available

LOC01   *Swindon's War Record* prepared by W.D. Bavin (1922) 2016 facsimile reprint.

This book is dedicated to the memory of
GORDON WILLIAM COLE
20 May 1897 – 1 July 1916

CONTENTS

Acknowledgements	vi
Introduction	vii
Sources	ix
Roll of Honour	1
Prisoners of War	109
Gallantry Awards and Medals	145

ACKNOWLEDGEMENTS

This book was prompted by an enquiry from Bert Evans which highlighted the lack of a World War Two Roll of Honour for the Swindon area. He has always been very supportive of this project, shown great interest in its progress and has supplied many useful pieces of information.

Many other members of the public have been very generous in sharing their family memories and research.

The Commonwealth War Graves Commission provided details of servicemen and women whose records contained the word 'Swindon'. This captured information on casualties that was not found in any other sources.

Members of *Swindon Heritage* magazine were interested in this project from the beginning and have assisted greatly in publicising the work. This has helped ensure the widest possible audience prior to publishing, in an attempt to ensure that all individuals are included.

Duncan and Mandy Ball's collection of photographs (www.oodwooc.co.uk) proved an invaluable source of information, and their assistance is very much appreciated.

Thanks go to Jon Ratcliffe for his photography, and especially to Darryl Moody, without whose practical support and encouragement this project would never have been completed.

INTRODUCTION

The centenary of the First World War has brought the events of 100 years ago into everyone's living room. We are all familiar with the images of exhausted soldiers, blighted landscapes and unending rows of neat white headstones. We have been told about the impact of that war on every aspect of life and how towns, cities and villages lost a generation of men.

However, the local story of the Second World War can seem less well documented: four years ago I was asked how many Swindon men died during that conflict and I had to admit that there was no known record. After the First World War, Swindon Council commissioned local headmaster William D. Bavin to write a history of the war and its effects on the town, resulting in the landmark publication 'Swindon's War Record' (1922). However, it seems nothing comparable was ever commissioned after 1945. The names, numbers and details of servicemen (and a few women) from Swindon and surrounding villages who gave their lives between 1939 and 1945 have never been counted. This is an attempt to correct that omission.

It is a simple idea: compile a database of servicemen and women from Swindon who were killed in World War Two. Simple in theory, but once started there are immediate questions to be answered. What constitutes a '*Swindonian*'; born here, lived here, family living here etc.? Which villages should be included? How about civilians? The criteria finally decided upon was that any serviceman or woman who had a connection with the parishes that now constitute the Borough of Swindon and the surrounding area would be included. In some cases the connection would be very strong, e.g. born and lived in the town, but for other men it may be more tenuous, e.g. married a Swindon woman. However any connection is relevant and such men should be remembered.

Owing to the scale of the project, no attempt has been made to include a biography of each entry. This is primarily an index of names, listing the sources for further research. Also recorded are details of prisoners of war (Section 2) and gallantry medals and awards (Section 3).

This is an ongoing project and we may never know the name of everyone who died. So far I have compiled a database with the following information:-

- 623 service personnel are listed having given their lives in the conflict.
- This number includes men (and 5 women) from all three services, (RAF, Royal Navy and British Army), regular soldiers, conscripts, reservists, nurses and the Home Guard.
- Their ages range from two Royal Navy sailors aged 17 to a 57 year old veteran.
- They served in every field of conflict throughout this truly 'world war', and also in every major battlefield; e.g. Battle of Britain, Monte Cassino, the fall of Singapore, Dunkirk, D-Day, North Africa etc.
- Some were killed in action, some died of wounds, and others were killed in accidents or died in prisoner of war camps.
- There are 9 sets of brothers.
- 221 men are listed as prisoners of war, from camps as far afield as Italy, Germany, Thailand and Burma. There will undoubtedly be many more whose names were not locally recorded. 11 of these died in the camps.
- Details were also found of 137 servicemen awarded gallantry medals or awards from all services and fields of combat. Of these, 22 men died during the war.

This work is ongoing and as any new resources come to light they will be researched. There will undoubtedly be men who are not listed in the sources, but who made the ultimate sacrifice. To our knowledge, this is the only Roll of Honour for Swindon and shows the impact of the war on one small town and how its men and women served across the world, in every major battlefield and in every service.

Katherine Cole
Local Studies, Swindon Central Library
November 2017

SOURCES

This research is based on the following list of sources. These either form part of the Local Studies collection (held at Swindon Central Library) or are available online.

The Commonwealth War Graves Commission (CWGC) has created an online casualty database which lists the 1.7 million men and women of the Commonwealth forces who died during the two world wars. The range of dates used by the CWGC to indicate death during World War Two are 3.09.1939 – 31.12.1947. They kindly sent me an extracted list of all World War Two casualty records that contained the word "Swindon". As this included *any* reference to 'Swindon', (e.g. Richard Swindon or Swindon, Gloucestershire), this required further examination to extract the servicemen from the local area. Local Studies held similar lists extracted from the CWGC for Blunsdon and Stratton St. Margaret. For any entry in the following Roll of Honour, I have noted the source as CWGC only where no other source has been found.

Cemeteries have been listed only where servicemen are buried in the Swindon area. Schools attended in the Swindon area are listed where known.

While it is beyond the scope of this project to verify the information listed in the sources, discrepancies between these sources have been highlighted.

Despite my best intentions, a project of this scale is surely going to contain errors. I welcome any corrections, omissions or suggestions. Please contact Local Studies if you find someone is missing or if you can help improve the accuracy of an entry.

Newspapers & Periodicals:

Title	*Range of dates searched*
Baptist Tabernacle magazine	1939 - 1945
Commonweal School Magazine	1939 – 1947
The Euclidean	1939 - 1946
Evening Advertiser	August 1939 - August 1945

Great Western Railway staff magazine   August 1939 - August 1946
Headlandian (Headlands School)   1945 - 1946
Highworth Link magazine
London Gazette
North Wilts Herald   Aug 1939- Aug 1945
Swindon Borough Council minutes   1939 - 1945
Swindonian   1939 - 1945
Wills Works Magazine   Aug 1945 & 1946

Books:

Fuller, Frederick W. *Build me an Ark: History of St. Saviour's Church* (Swindon: *Crossfire*, 1996).
In Memoriam [WW2 casualties from Swindon Press staff] (Swindon: Swindon Press, 1946).
Millennium Memories (Swindon: ELSP, 2000)
Wroughton History Group – Book 7: *Wroughton through to the 60s (1997)*
Wroughton History Group – Book 8: *Wroughton in Pictures 1945-2002* (2002)
Wroughton History Group – Book 9: *Stories from Wroughton* (2009)
Wroughton History Group - Book 10: *Reflections of Wroughton during the two World Wars* (2016).

Online Resources:

Commonwealth War Graves Commission (CWGC):
   www.cwgc.org.uk
Duncan and Mandy:
   www.oodwooc.co.uk/Index.htm
Highworth Historical Society:
   www.highworthhistoricalsociety.co.uk
WW2 Talk:
   ww2talk.com/forums/topic/14292-swindon-scouts-memorial/
Hut Six:
   www.hut-six.co.uk

War Memorials:

- Bishopstone
- Blunsdon
- Broad Hinton
- Christ Church (Swindon)
- Gorse Hill Working Man's Club memorial (now inside the chapel at Radnor Street Cemetery)
- Highworth
- Lydiard Millicent
- Purton
- Sanford Street Congregational Church font
- South Marston
- St. Augustine (Swindon)
- St. Mary (Purton)
- Swindon Post Office Memorial
- Swindon Scouts Memorial
- Wanborough
- Wroughton
- Wiltshire Constabulary Memorial, Devizes

ROLL OF HONOUR

A

ABELL
WILLIAM HENRY
ROYAL ARTILLERY
- Private
- Age: 24
- Died: 30.06.1944

Source: *Evening Advertiser* 08.07.1944, p.4 (photo)

ACKLING
ALBERT F.
ROYAL NAVY (HMS Duke)
- Petty Officer Telegraphist
- Age: 26
- Died: 09.07.1943
- Buried in Whitworth Road Cemetery, Swindon

Source: CWGC

ACKLING
FREDERICK GEORGE
ROYAL ARTILLERY
- Bombardier
- Age: 29
- Died: 27.12.1945
- Buried in Highworth Cemetery

Source: CWGC

ADAMS
DESMOND
DORSETSHIRE REGIMENT / 6 COMMANDO
- Private
- Age: 19
- Died: 06.06.1944
- Son of Stanley and Daisy Adams of Wanborough

Source: CWGC

ADAMS
JACK HOWARD
YEOMANRY REGIMENT
- Gunner
- Age: 20
- Died: 20.05.1944
- Killed at Monte Cassino

Source: 'Build me an Ark', *Crossfire*, 1996, p.109
North Wilts Herald 09.06.1944, p.8 (photo)
Evening Advertiser 03.06.1944, p.1 (photo)
Evening Advertiser 22.05.1945, p.2

ALEXANDER
RONALD CHARLES
ROYAL AIR FORCE Voluntary Reserve
- Aircraftman 2nd class
- Age: 23
- Died: 15.12.1940
- Attended Clarence Street School

Source: *North Wilts Herald* 24.01.1941, p.8 (photo)
Evening Advertiser 21.01.41, p.3 (photo)

ALEXANDER
WILLIAM THOMAS EDWARD
PARACHUTE REGIMENT AAC
- Private
- Age: 23
- Died: 03.07.1945
- Accidentally drowned while canoeing on the Thames at Oxford
- Buried in Highworth Cemetery

Source: www.highworthhistoricalsociety.co.uk
Highworth War Memorial

ALEY
WILLIAM HARRY
CAMERONIANS
- Corporal
- Age: 24
- Died: 01.10.1944

Source: CWGC

ALLCOCK
ALFRED GEORGE
ROYAL ARMY SERVICE CORPS
- Driver
- Died: 24.11.1943

Source: CWGC

ALLDIS
STANLEY
ROYAL NAVY (HMS Wrestler)
- Able Seaman
- Age: 36
- Died: 30.10.1941

Source: CWGC

ALLEN
F.R.
Source: Gorse Hill Working Men's Club memorial, in Radnor Street Cemetery Chapel, Swindon

ALLEN
THOMAS WILLIAM (WILL)
ROYAL ARTILLERY
- Gunner
- Age: 32
- Died: 27.05.1942
- Attended Sanford Street School

Source: *North Wilts Herald* 26.06.1942, p.5 (photo)
Evening Advertiser 23.06.1942, p.1 (photo)
Evening Advertiser 28.05.1943, p.2
Evening Advertiser 27.05.1944, p.2

ALLNAT
EDWARD ERNEST
ROYAL AIR FORCE Voluntary Reserve
- Flight Sergeant
- Age: 23
- Died: 18.04.1941
- Attended Sanford Street School
- Family information states he worked at Monahan's. A telegraph reported him missing 18.04.1941, confirmed missing presumed killed, 11.12.1941

Source: *North Wilts Herald* 06.02.1942, p.5
Evening Advertiser 02.02.1942, p.1 (photo)

ANDERSON
NORMAN MACLEOD
ROYAL AIR FORCE Voluntary Reserve
- Leading Aircraftman
- Age: 25
- Died: 17.11.1945
- Attended Wroughton School

Source: www.roll-of-honour.com/wiltshire/wroughton

ANDREWS
FREDERICK ARTHUR
QUEEN'S ROYAL REGIMENT
- Private
- Age: 21
- Died: 20.05.1940

Source: *Evening Advertiser* 23.08.2010, p.16
Evening Advertiser 24.06.1940, p.1 (photo)
Evening Advertiser 24.08.1940, p.3
North Wilts Herald 30.08.1940, p.4 (photo)
Great Western Railway Magazine January 1945, p.15

ANGEL
HERBERT HENRY
GLOUCESTER REGIMENT
- Private
- Age: 28
- Died: 14.06.1942
- Attended Sanford Street School

Source: *North Wilts Herald* 02.04.1943, p.8
Evening Advertiser 01.04.1943, p.5 (photo)
Evening Advertiser 14.06.1945, p.2

ARCHER
ALBERT GEORGE
WILTSHIRE REGIMENT
- Lance Corporal
- Age: 31
- Died: 17.03.1944
- Killed at Anzio

Source: Purton War Memorial

ARCHER
ALBERT JOHN OWEN
ROYAL AIR FORCE 207 Squadron Bomber Command
- Sergeant
- Age: 23
- Died: 30.01.1944
- Shot down during raid over Berlin

Source: Rodbourne Community History Group

ARKELL (MC and Bar)
JAMES WILLIAM
ROYAL GURKHA RIFLES
- Major
- Age: 25
- Died: 21.08.1946

Source: www.highworthhistoricalsociety.co.uk
Highworth War Memorial
North Wilts Herald 09.07.1943, p.7
North Wilts Herald 17.05.1944, p.4 (photo)
North Wilts Herald 18.08.1944, p.5 (photo)
Evening Advertiser 18.05.1944, pp.2 & 8 (photo)
Evening Advertiser 16.08.1944, p.4 (photo)
see Awards and Medals

ARMSTRONG
CHARLES
WILTSHIRE REGIMENT
- Private
- Age: 52
- 16.08.1944
- Buried in Whitworth Road Cemetery, Swindon

Source: CWGC

ARMSTRONG
ROBERT
ROYAL NAVY
- Chief Petty Officer
- Died 04.08.1940

Source: *Evening Advertiser* 22.08.1940, p.4
Evening Advertiser 05.08.1945, p.2

ARNOLD
CHARLES JAMES
ESSEX REGIMENT
- Private
- Age: 25
- Died: 31.07.1942
- Died of malaria in India

Source: *Evening Advertiser* 28.08.1942, p.1 (photo)
Evening Advertiser 31.07.1945, p.2

ASHTON
CECIL ROBERT
ROYAL ENGINEERS
- Lance Sergeant
- Age: 26
- Died: 06.06.1941
- Killed on Juno beach on D Day

Source: www.highworthhistoricalsociety.co.uk
Highworth War Memorial

ASHTON
STANLEY WILLIAM
ROYAL AIR FORCE
- Pilot Officer
- Age: 28
- Died: 04.06.1940
- Reported killed in aircraft accident
- Buried in Radnor Street Cemetery, Swindon

Source: *North Wilts Herald* 07.06.1940, p.5
Evening Advertiser 06.06.1940, p.1
Evening Advertiser 11.06.1940, p.4
Evening Advertiser 04.06.1945, p.2

ASHTON HILL
ROBERT
HONG KONG VOLUNTEER DEFENCE FORCE
- Lance Corporal
- Age: 44
- Died: 27.09.1944
- Husband of Ruth Emily Hill, of Swindon

Source: CWGC

ASTLE (DFC)
ALFRED (FREDDIE)
ROYAL AIR FORCE Voluntary Reserve
- Pilot Officer
- Age: 29
- Died: 24.09.1944
- Missing after an operation in France
- Was a Police Constable before enlisting

Source: *North Wilts Herald* 03.03.1944, p.4
Evening Advertiser 04.10.1944, p.4 (photo)
Wiltshire Constabulary Memorial, London Road, Devizes
See Awards & Medals

AVENELL
JOSEPH HENRY
GLOUCESTER REGIMENT
- Private
- Age: 21
- Died: 05.05.1942

Source:CWGC

AXTON
JOHN OWEN
ROYAL NAVY
- Able Seaman
- Age: 20
- Died: 17.03.1944
- Attended Upper Stratton School

Source:*North Wilts Herald* 31.03.1944, p.5
Evening Advertiser 13.04.1944, p.2 (photo)

B

**BAKER
RONALD JAMES**
ROYAL NAVY
- Engine Room Artificer 4th Class
- Age: 23
- Died: 07.11.1944

Source: CWGC

**BALDWIN
FREDERICK STANLEY**
ROYAL ARTILLERY
- Gunner
- Age: 19
- Died: 21.07.1944

Source: Coleshill War Memorial
www.highworthhistoricalsociety.co.uk

**BARKHAM
ALBERT REGINALD**
ROYAL ARTILLERY
- Gunner
- Age: 21
- Died: 09.10.1943
- Brother of **RONALD BARKHAM** below
- *Evening Advertiser* names him Albert Edward
- Family information states he died in Italy, near Campobasso

Source: *Great Western Railway Magazine* January 1944, p.16
Evening Advertiser 15.11.1943, p.3

**BARKHAM
DOUGLAS ANTHONY**
ROYAL AIR FORCE
- Leading Aircraftman
- Age: 20
- CWGC lists age as 21
- Died: 24.03.1941
- Not brother of Albert and Ronald Barkham also listed
- Brother **FREDERICK BARKHAM** escaped POW camp in Italy, see Prisoners of War

Source: *Evening Advertiser* 27.03.1941
Evening Advertiser 16.10.1943, p.5
Evening Advertiser 24.3.1944, p.2

**BARKHAM
RONALD JOHN**
ROYAL AIR FORCE Voluntary Reserve
- Sergeant
- Age: 20
- Died: 06.02.1943
- Brother of **ALBERT BARKHAM** above
- Family information state he left RAF Leuchars on a mission over coast of Norway, and never returned

Source: CWGC

**BARNES
ALBERT JAMES**
ROYAL NAVY (HMS Neptune)
- Chief Stoker
- Age: 41
- Died: 19.12.1941

Source: CWGC

BARRETT
ALBERT REGINALD
ROYAL NAVY (HMS Eagle)
- Engine Room Artificer 3rd Class
- Age: 32
- Died: 11.08.1942

Source: *Evening Advertiser* 11.08.1945, p.2

BARTHOLOMEW
JOHN FREDERICK
ROYAL AIR FORCE
Aircraftsman 2nd Class
- Age: 19
- Died: 06.01.1945
- Killed in flying accident in England.
- Attended Euclid Street School, Swindon

Source: *North Wilts Herald* 12.01.1945, p.5 (photo)
Headlandian Summer 1945, p.22
Headlandian Summer 1946, p.30

BATHE
HARRY ERNEST
ROYAL NAVY (HMS Hermes)
- Chief Engineroom Artificer
- Age: 53
- Died: 09.04.1942
- Son served in Royal Air Force
- Licensee of the Running Horse pub, Swindon

Source: *North Wilts Herald* 15.05.1942, p.3 (photo)
Evening Advertiser 11.05.1942, p.1 (photo)

BEAMES
FREDERICK WILLIAM
ROYAL ENGINEERS
- Lance Corporal
- Age: 32
- Died 17.06.1940
- Died on the R.M.S. Lancastria
- Attended Clifton Street School, Swindon

Source: *Great Western Railway Magazine* October 1946, p.228
North Wilts Herald 05.09.1941, pp.4-5 (photo)
Evening Advertiser 23.07.1940, p.1 (photo)
Evening Advertiser 03.09.1941, p.2 (photo

BEASANT
RICHARD
WORCESTERSHIRE REGIMENT
- Corporal
- Age: 21
- Died: between 29.05.1940 - 08.06.1940

Source: Lydiard Millicent War Memorial

BENFIELD (Mentioned in Despatches)
VICTOR HAROLD
ROYAL AIR FORCE
- Flight Sergeant
- Age: 24
- Died: 19.06.1943
- Attended Swindon Secondary School

Source: *Swindonian* Summer 1943, p.922
Evening Advertiser 20.06.1945, p.2

BENNETT
CLARENCE ANTHONY
ROYAL AIR FORCE Voluntary Reserve
- Aircraftman 2nd class
- Age: 35
- Died: 29.05.1942

Source: CWGC

BERG
WILLIAM HENRY
ROYAL WELCH FUSILIERS
- Fusilier
- Age: 27
- Died: 07.10.1942
- Buried in Chiseldon cemetery

Source: CWGC

BERRY
JOHN JAMES
ROYAL AIR FORCE Voluntary Reserve
- Sergeant
- Age: 21
- Died: 13.08.1941

Source: CWGC

BEVINGTON
LAWRENCE ERNEST
ROYAL NAVAL RESERVE (HMS Rawalpindi)
- Acting Sub Lieutenant
- Died: 23.11.1939
- While on patrol between Iceland and the Faroes HMS Rawalpindi was attacked by the German battle cruisers Scharnhorst and Gneisenau
- Attended Euclid Street School, Swindon

Source: *Evening Advertiser* 23.11.2009, p.16
St Augustine Church memorial
Evening Advertiser 29.11.1939, p.1 (photo)
ww2talk.com/forums

BEWLEY
EDWARD WILLIAM
CARPENTER (TED)
ROYAL AIR FORCE
- Flight Sergeant
- Age: 25
- Died: 27.05.1943
- Died in POW camp in Java

Source: CWGC
Evening Advertiser 29.05.1944, p.2
See Prisoners Of War

BICKFORD (DSO)
EDWARD OSCAR
ROYAL NAVY (HM Sub Salmon)
- Commander
- Died: 14.07.1940
- Born at Purton
- Killed when submarine was sunk

Source: *North Wilts Herald* 14.07.1940, p.5
Evening Advertiser 22.07.1940, p.1 (photo)

BILL
WILLIAM JAMES
ROYAL AIR FORCE
- Sergeant Wireless Mechanic/Air Gunner
- Age: 27
- Died: 21.11.1943
- Buried in Whitworth Road Cemetery, Swindon

Source: CWGC

BISHOP
HENRY BARTLETT
ROYAL AIR FORCE
- Corporal
- Died: 06.11.1942

Source: *Great Western Railway Magazine* January 1943, p.12
Buried in Radnor Street Cemetery, Swindon

BIZLEY
EDWARD WILLIAM
ROYAL NAVY (HMS Algerine)
- Engine Room Artificer 2nd Class
- Age: 30
- Died: 15.11.1942

Source: CWGC

BLACKALL
HAROLD WILLIAM
ROYAL ELECTRICAL AND MECHANICAL ENGINEERS
- Warrant Officer
- Age: 40
- Died: 01.03.1943
- Died in the Indian Base General Hospital, Poona

Source: *Great Western Railway Magazine* May 1943, p.76
15 Shop Memorial, STEAM, Swindon
Evening Advertiser 08.03.1943, p.2

BLAKE
TERENCE DAVID BRIAN
ROYAL AIR FORCE
- Flight Lieutenant (Pilot)
- Age: 29
- Died: 13.09.1943

Source: *North Wilts Herald* 01.10.1943, p.6 (photo)

BLAKENEY
ALBERT
ROYAL NAVY (HMS BARHAM)
- Ordinary Seaman
- Age: 26
- Died: 25.11.1941

Source: War memorial in St Mary's Church, Purton

BLAYLOCK
DAVID
ROYAL ENGINEERS
- Sapper
- Died: 13.04.1945
- Attended Euclid Street School, Swindon

Source:*Headlandian* Summer 1945, p.22
Headlandian Summer 1946, p.30

BLOCK
ALBERT LEWIS
RIFLE BRIGADE
- Corporal
- Age: 27
- Died: 17.05.1944
- Died at Monte Cassino

Source:CWGC

BLUNSDON
FRANK HENRY
MERCHANT NAVY (SS Port Darwin)
- Ordinary Seaman
- Died: 10.10.1947
- Buried in Whitworth Road Cemetery, Swindon

Source:CWGC

BOND
ALFRED JOHN
ROYAL MARINES
- Lance Corporal
- Age: 24
- Died: 06.12.1944
- Attended Rodbourne Cheney School, Swindon

Source:*Great Western Railway Magazine* February 1945, p.32
Evening Advertiser 08.12.1944, p.2

BOND
EDGAR
NORFOLK REGIMENT
- Private
- Age: 25
- Died: 11.02.1942

Source:CWGC

BOND
EDWARD
NORFOLK REGIMENT
- Private
- Age: 26
- Died: 09.09.1943

Source: CWGC

BOND
LESLIE
DORSET REGIMENT
- Private
- Age: 22
- Died: 11.06.1944
- Attended Wroughton Senior School

Source:*Great Western Railway Magazine* September 1944, p.143
North Wilts Herald 14.07.1944, p.8 (photo)
Evening Advertiser 10.07.1944, p.4 (photo)
Wroughton History Group - Book 10 (2016) p.73

BONNER
JOSEPH
SEAFORTH HIGHLANDERS
- Private
- Age: 31
- Died: 02.06.1940

Source: *Evening Advertiser* 14.06.2010, p.17
North Wilts Herald 21.06.1940, p.8
Evening Advertiser 17.06.1940, p.1

**BONNER
COLIN ABBOTT**
ROYAL NAVY (HMS Hood)
- Able Seaman
- Died: 24.05.1941
- Parents lived at Westrop House, Highworth

Source: www.highworthhistoricalsociety.co.uk
Highworth War Memorial

**BONNEY
WILLIAM GEORGE**
ROYAL FUSILIERS (City of London Regiment)
- Corporal
- Age: 32
- Died: 05.06.1940

Source:CWGC

**BOON
GORDON M**
ROYAL AIR FORCE
- Flight Sergeant Pilot
- Age: 21
- Died: 11.12.1943
- Attended Commonweal School, Swindon

Source:*Commonweal School Magazine* Summer 1944, p.6
Evening Advertiser 28.12.1943, p.2

**BORMAN
REGIONALD PATRICK**
ROYAL ARTILLERY
- Gunner
- Age: 34
- Died: 06.08.1944

Source: Wroughton War Memorial
North Wilts Herald 15.09.1944, p.5 (photo)
Evening Advertiser 11.09.1944, p.4 (photo)
Wroughton History Group - Book 10 (2016), p.73

**BOTSFORD
ARCHIBALD GRAHAM**
ROYAL ENGINEERS
- Lieutenant
- Died: 20.03.1941
- Buried in Highworth Cemetery

Source:CWGC

**BOUCHER
NORMAN HUGH**
ARMY CATERING CORPS
- Private
- Age: 28
- Died: 07.06.1944
- Buried in Whitworth Road Cemetery, Swindon

Source:CWGC

**BOWERING
HEDLEY**
ROYAL AIR FORCE Voluntary Reserve
- Leading Aircraftman
- Age: 23
- Died: 11.12.1942
- Died in a motorbike accident in Alton
- Buried in Wroughton Cemetery

Source:*Great Western Railway Magazine* February 1943, p.29
Wroughton War Memorial
Evening Advertiser 19.12.1942, p.6
Evening Advertiser 11.12.1944, p.2
Wroughton History Group - Book 10 (2016), p.73

BOWLES
EDWARD G
ROYAL FUSILIERS (City of London Regiment)
- Fusilier
- Age: 30
- Died: 06.09.1944

Source: South Marston War Memorial

BRADLEY
ARTHUR WILLIAM
WILTSHIRE REGIMENT/ ROYAL ULSTER RIFLES
- Corporal
- Age: 28
- Died: 17.09.1944

Source: *Great Western Railway Magazine* December 1944, p.193
North Wilts Herald 20.10.1944, p.8 (photo)
Evening Advertiser 13.10.1944, p.4 (photo)
Evening Advertiser 18.09.45, p.2

BRADNUM
GEORGE WILLIAM
ROYAL ENGINEERS
- Sapper
- Age: 24
- Died: 30.03.1943

Source: CWGC

BRASSINGTON
NORMAN FREDERICK
ROYAL AIR FORCE
- Sergeant Wireless Operator/Air Gunner
- Age: 26
- Died: 15.09.1942

Source: 'In Memoriam,' 1946 Swindon Press (photo)
North Wilts Herald 25.09.1942, p.4 (photo)
Evening Advertiser 18.09.1942, p.1 (photo)

BRIDGMAN
MERVYN DENNIS
ROYAL NAVY (HMS Trinidad)
- Engineroom Artificer
- Died: 14.05.1942
- Attended Gorse Hill School, Swindon

Source: *Great Western Railway Magazine* August 1942, p.149
Evening Advertiser 16.06.1942, p.4 (photo)
Evening Advertiser 15.5.1944, p.2
Evening Advertiser 14.05.1945, p.2
Evening Advertiser 21.05.1945, p.3

BRIDGES
ARTHUR GERALD DAVID
WILTSHIRE REGIMENT
- Private
- Age: 21
- Died: 06.08.1944

Source: Wroughton War Memorial
Wroughton History Group - Book 10 (2016) p.73

BRIDGES
GORDON LESLIE
WILTSHIRE REGIMENT
- Private
- Age: 18
- Died: 12.07.1944

Source: *Evening Advertiser* 13.07.1945, p.2

BRIND
?
ROYAL ENGINEERS
- Sapper
- Age: 24
- Died of wounds
- Attended Aldbourne School

Source: *Evening Advertiser* 06.09.1944, p.5 (photo)

BRISTOW
WILLIAM FREDERICK
ROYAL ARTILLERY/ 7 Commando
- Gunner/Lance Bombardier
- Age: 24
- Died: 15.07.1941

Source: *Evening Advertiser* 14.07.1945, p.2
Evening Advertiser 16.07.1945, p.2

BROOKS
CHARLES LEVERSON
ROYAL NAVY (HMS Courageous)
- Engine Room Artificer
- Age: 51
- Died: 17.09.1939
- Brother of **HARRY BROOKS** (below)
- This was the only time they had served on the same ship

Source: *Evening Advertiser* 21.09.1939, p.1 (photo)

BROOKS
HARRY THOMAS
ROYAL NAVY (HMS Courageous)
- Engine Room Artificer
- Age: 45
- Died: 17.09.1939
- Brother of **CHARLES BROOKS** (above)
- This was the only time they had served on the same ship

Source: *Evening Advertiser* 21.09.1939, p1 (photo)

BROOKS
JACK
ROYAL ARMY MEDICAL CORPS/ PARACHUTE REGIMENT
- Private
- Age: 22
- Died: 24.03.1945

Source: *Great Western Railway Magazine* July 1945, p.116
North Wilts Herald 13.07.1945, p 4
Evening Advertiser 11.07.1945, p.2

BROWN
ALBERT GEORGE
ROYAL ARMY SERVICE CORPS
- Lance Corporal
- Age: 27
- Died: 24.06.1944
- Killed in action at sea while a POW of Japan
- Attended Highworth School

Source: www.highworthhistoricalsociety.co.uk
Highworth War Memorial
See Prisoners of War

BROWN
EDWIN ALBERT
WELCH REGIMENT
- Colour Sergeant
- Age: 25
- Died: 07.11.1946
- Buried in Whitworth Road Cemetery, Swindon

Source: CWGC

BROWN
GODFREY ALLISON
ROYAL AIR FORCE Voluntary Reserve
- Squadron Leader
- Age: 33
- Died: 19.12.1942
- Lost over the Atlantic

Source: *Evening Advertiser* 18.12.1943, p.2

BROWN
RAYMOND JOHN
ROYAL SUSSEX REGIMENT
- Private
- Age: 22
- Died: 22.08.1944

Source: *Great Western Railway Magazine* November 1944, p.175

BROWN
REGINALD GEORGE
ROYAL AIR FORCE
- Wireless Operator/Gunner
- Age: 21
- Died: 29.01.1944
- Attended Chiseldon School

Source: *Evening Advertiser* 07.09.44, p.2 (photo)

BRYAN
WILLIAM
Source: *North Wilts Herald* 15.09.1944, p.4
Evening Advertiser 26.08.1944, p.5 (photo)
Evening Advertiser 02.09.1944, p.3 (photo)

BRYANT
CECIL NORMAN
ROYAL NAVY (HMS Suffolk)
- Able Seaman
- Age: 23
- Died: 10.02.1940

Source: CWGC

BRYANT
LESLIE FRANCIS
ROYAL ENGINEERS
- Sapper
- Age: 23
- Died: 16.11.1943
- Son of Regier Frank and Jane Louise Bryant, of Highworth

Source: CWGC

BUCKLAND
WILLIAM HENRY
ROYAL AIR FORCE Voluntary Reserve
- Leading Aircraftman
- Age: 29
- Died: 30.08.1944
- Buried in Whitworth Road Cemetery, Swindon

Source: Memorial in St Augustine's Church, Swindon

**BURGESS
JOHN HOWARD**
ROYAL NAVY (HM Sub Salmon)
- Able Seaman
- Reported missing after sinking of submarine

Source:*Evening Advertiser* 22.07.1940, p.1 (photo)

**BURGESS
WALTER ARTHUR (NIBBY)**
ROYAL AIR FORCE Voluntary Reserve
- Sergeant Navigator
- Age: 20
- Died: 24.08.1943
- Died in a plane crash in Cairo
- Attended Euclid Street School, Swindon

Source: *The Euclidean* Christmas 1943
Great Western Railway Magazine November 1943, p.172
North Wilts Herald 07.10.1943, p2 (photo)
Headlandian Summer 1946, p.30
ww2talk.com/forums

**BURGOYNE
REGINALD WILLIAM ARTHUR**
ROYAL NAVY (HMS Lanka)
- Engine Room Artificer 5th Class
- Died: 12.02.1944

Source:CWGC

**BURTON
WILLIAM JAMES**
GLOUCESTER REGIMENT
- Lance Corporal
- Age: 29
- Died: 28.09.1942
- Died as the result of an accident in India

Source:*Great Western Railway Magazine* January 1943, p.12
North Wilts Herald 16.10.1942, p.5 (photo)
Evening Advertiser 14.10.1942, p.4 (photo)

**BUTLER
LESLIE JOHN**
ROYAL TANK REGIMENT
- Trooper
- Age: 26
- Died: 22.03.1943
- Attended Gorse Hill School, Swindon

Source:*North Wilts Herald* 09.04.1943, p.4 (photo)
North Wilts Herald 07.04.1943, p.4 (photo)

**BUTLER
STANLEY Ernest**
ROYAL NAVY (HMS Illustrious)
- Petty Officer
- Age: 24
- Died: 10.01.41

Source: *Evening Advertiser* 29.01.1941, p.4

BUTLIN
DUDLEY OWEN
RECONNAISSANCE CORPS
- Lieutenant
- Age: 22
- Died: 13.04.1945
- Attended Swindon High School, Swindon

Source:*North Wilts Herald* 01.09.1944, p.2 (photo)
'Build me an Ark', *Crossfire*, 1996, p.109
Evening Advertiser 23.01.1945, p.8 (photo)
Christ Church War Memorial, Swindon

BUXTON
CYRIL ERNEST
WILTSHIRE REGIMENT
- Private
- Age: 21
- Died: 26.08.1944
- Attended Sanford Street School, Swindon

Source:*North Wilts Herald* 06.10.1944, p.5
Evening Advertiser 13.09.1944, p.3 (photo)
Evening Advertiser 16.01.1945, p.4

C

CANN
STANLEY EDGAR THOMAS
ROYAL MARINES
- Marine
- Age: 43
- Died: 21.08.1943
- Buried in Lower Stratton Cemetery

Source: CWGC

CARD
ARTHUR STANLEY
WILTSHIRE REGIMENT/
QUEENS OWN ROYAL WEST KENT REGIMENT
- Private
- Age: 21
- Died: 18.09.1944
- Brother of **PERCY** and **WILLIAM CARD** see below

Source: *Great Western Railway Magazine* December 1944, p.192
Wroughton War Memorial
North Wilts Herald 01.09.1944
Evening Advertiser 05.10.1944, p.5 (photo);
Wroughton History Group - Book 10 (2016), p.74

CARD
PERCY GEORGE
ROYAL NAVY (HMS Albatross)
- Acting Leading Signalman
- Age: 20
- Died: 18.08.1944
- Attended Wroughton School
- Brother of **ARTHUR** and **WILLIAM CARD**

Source: *North Wilts Herald* 29.09.1944, p.8 (photo
Evening Advertiser 28.08.1944, p.8 (photo)
Evening Advertiser 05.10.1944, p.5 (photo)

CARD
WILLIAM FREDERICK
ROYAL ARTILLERY
- Gunner
- Age: 35
- Died: 05.03.1943
- Brother of **PERCY** and **ARTHUR CARD** see above

Source: *Great Western Railway Magazine* August 1946, p.183
19D Shop Memorial, STEAM, Swindon
Evening Advertiser 05.10.1944, p.5 (photo)
Wroughton History Book 10, p.74

CARNELL
RICHARD JAMES
ROYAL ARMOURED CORPS
- Trooper
- Age: 31
- Died: 4.09.1944

Source: *Evening Advertiser*
02.09.1944, p.8

CARPENTER
ERNEST WILLIAM
ROYAL AIR FORCE
- Corporal
- Age: 32
- Died: 03.08.1943
- Attended Wroughton School

Source: *North Wilts Herald*
13.08.1943, p.4 (photo)
Evening Advertiser 11.08.1943, p.8 (photo)
Evening Advertiser 03.08.1945, p.2
Wroughton History Group - Book 10 (2016), p.74

CARTER (DFC)
ALBERT LESLIE
ROYAL AIR FORCE
- Squadron Leader (Navigator)
- Age: 29
- Died: 23.12.1944

Source: Wroughton War Memorial
North Wilts Herald 06.04.1945, p.5
Evening Advertiser 02.04.1945, p.5
Evening Advertiser 09.04.1945, p.2
Evening Advertiser 05.10.1945, p.4
Wroughton History Group - Book 10 (2016), pp.75 & 102
See Awards and Medals

CARTER
ERNEST JOSEPH
DUKE OF CORNWALL'S LIGHT INFANTRY
- Private
- Age: 28
- Died: 27.06.1944
- Attended Westcott Place School, Swindon

Source: *North Wilts Herald*
28.07.1944, p.5 (photo)
Evening Advertiser 26.07.1944, p.2 (photo)
Evening Advertiser 27.06.1945, p.2

CARTER
ROGER GRAHAM
ROYAL ARTILLERY
- Gunner
- Died: 17.01.1941
- Buried in Purton (St Mary) Cemetery
- Parents ran the Station Stores, Purton

Source: *Evening Advertiser*
22.01.1941, p.4
Evening Advertiser 17.01.44, p.2

CASEY
SIDNEY
ROYAL MARINES
- Marine
- Age: 21
- Died: 28.08.1941
- Died while POW in Germany from gunshot wound in left side of head

Source: *North Wilts Herald*
10.10.1941, p.2
See Prisoners of War

CASTLE
ARTHUR EDGAR JOHN
ROYAL ARTILLERY
- Gunner
- Age: 22
- Died: 01.03.1944

Source: *Great Western Railway Magazine* May 1944, p.82

CASWELL
WALTER
ROYAL ENGINEERS
- Corporal
- Age: 43
- Died: 08.05.1944
- Buried in Upper Stratton Cemetery, Swindon

Source: CWGC

CHAPLIN
HENRY LEOPOLD
PIONEER CORPS
- Private
- Age: 22
- Died: 13.04.1943

Source: CWGC

CHEESLEY
DAVID JESSE (JESSE)
6th AIRBORNE DIVISION
- Lance Corporal
- Died: 01.04.1945
- Attended Even Swindon School, Swindon

Source: *North Wilts Herald* 27.04.1945, p.8 (photo)
St Augustine War Memorial
www.highworthhistoricalsociety.co.uk
Highworth War Memorial

CHITTOCK
ISAIAH LEWIS
ROYAL AIR FORCE Voluntary Reserve
- Sergeant Air Gunner
- Age: 24

Died: 25.05.1944
Source: CWGC

CHURCH
JOHN PHILIP HAROLD
MILITARY POLICE
- Lance Corporal
- Age: 36
- Died: 21.07.1944

Source: *Evening Advertiser* 07.08.1944, p.4
Evening Advertiser 21.07.1945, p.2

CLARIDGE
HUBERT VICTOR
PIONEER CORPS
- Private
- Age: 21
- Died: 29.10.1944
- Attended Shrivenham School

Source: *North Wilts Herald* 10.11.1944, p.4 (photo)

CLARK
NORMAN VICTOR
FLEET AIR ARM
- Sub-Lieutenant
- Died: 24.02.1942
- Attended Commonweal School, Swindon

Source: *Commonweal School Magazine* Summer 1942, p.3

CLARK
STANLEY LEONARD
WILTSHIRE REGIMENT/
DUKE OF CORNWALL'S
LIGHT INFANTRY
- Private
- Age: 37
- Died: 11.07.1944
- Attended Westcott Place School, Swindon

Source: *Great Western Railway Magazine* September 1944, p.143
St Augustine Church Memorial
North Wilts Herald 18.08.1944, p.3
Evening Advertiser 16.08.1944, p.2

CLAUGHAN
GEOFFREY PERCIVAL
ROYAL NAVY (HMS Victorious)
- Leading Airman
- Age: 20
- Died: 14.04.1945
- Missing in action with Fleet Air Arm on island between Japan and Formosa

Source: *Evening Advertiser* 23.05.1945, p.2

CLINTON MBE
GILBERT JAMES
MERCHANT NAVY (SS Tucurinca)
- Third Engineer Officer
- Age: 52
- Died: 11.03.1943

Source: CWGC
See Awards and Medals

CODRINGTON
WILLIAM ALEXANDER ROBERT
COLDSTREAM GUARDS
- 2nd Lieutenant
- Age: 21
- Died: 14.03.1941

Source: Wroughton War Memorial
Wroughton History Group - Book 10 (2016), p.75

COLBY
GEORGE
ROYAL ARMY SERVICE CORPS
- Driver
- Age: 33
- Died: 23.08.1944
- Buried in Chiseldon Cemetery

Source: CWGC

COLE
H. W. (FRANK)
ROYAL ARTILLERY
- Gunner/Driver
- Age: 25
- Died: 30.04.1945
- Attended Ferndale Road School, Swindon

Source: *Great Western Railway Magazine* August 1945, p.132
Evening Advertiser 14.05.1945, p.1 (photo)
Evening Advertiser 15.05.1945, p.2

COLLETT
LEONARD STANLEY
ROYAL NAVY (HMS Blean)
- Able Seaman
- Age: 20
- Died: 11.12.1942
- HMS Blean was sunk by U433

Source: St Barnabas memorial plaque, St Barnabas Church, Swindon
Gorse Hill Working Man's Club plaque, Radnor Street Cemetery, Swindon

COLLINGBORN
FRANCIS WILLIAM BERNARD
TANK REGIMENT
- Trooper
- Age: 27
- Died: 21.07.1943
- Attended Commonweal School, Swindon

Source: *Commonweal School Mag* Summer 1944, p.5,

COLLINS
LESLIE ROWLAND
ROYAL ARMOURED CORPS
- Trooper
- Age: 20
- Died: 13.04.1945

Source: CWGC

COOK
WILFRED
TANK REGIMENT
- Attended Commonweal School, Swindon

Source: *Commonweal School Magazine* Summer 1946, p.4

COOLE
PAMELA CONSTANCE MARY
WOMEN'S ARMY AIR CORPS
- Leading Aircraftwoman
- Age: 17
- Died: 27.08.1944
- *Evening Advertiser* says her age was 18
- Daughter of Chief Motor Mechanic AF Coole, Royal Navy, formerly of Swindon

Source: *Evening Advertiser* 06.09.1944, p.2

COOPER
ANTHONY GORDON
FLEET AIR ARM (HMS Indefatigable)
- Sub Lieutenant
- Age: 19
- Died: 27.03.1945
- Attached to Pacific Task Force, off Japan
- Attended Commonweal School, Swindon

Source: *Commonweal School Magazine* Summer 1945, p.6
North Wilts Herald 20.04.1945, p.8 (photo)
Evening Advertiser 16.04.1945, p.2 (photo)

COOPER
KENNETH GEORGE
DORSET REGIMENT
- Private
- Age: 25
- Died: 24.03.1941
- Parents lived in Park Ave, Highworth

Source: www.highworthhistoricalsociety.co.uk
Highworth War Memorial

**CORNISH
A. F.**
ROYAL ARMY ORDNANCE CORPS
- Lance Corporal

Source: *Great Western Railway Magazine* December 1943, p.189

**COTTLE
KENNETH ARTHUR HENRY**
EAST SURREY REGIMENT
- Private
- Age: 26
- Died: 15.02.1942

Source: CWGC

**COULING
WALTER JOHN THOMAS**
ROYAL ARTILLERY
- Lance Bombardier
- Age: 29
- Died: 01.10.1943

Source: CWGC

**COURT
REGINALD**
MILITARY PROVOST STAFF CORPS
- Sergeant
- Age: 53
- Died: 01.12.1943
- Buried in Chiseldon Cemetery

Source: CWGC

**COUZENS
GARNETT**
ROYAL AIR FORCE
- Sergeant
- Age: 25
- Died: 24.02.1941
- Killed in a flying accident in Malaya
- Attended Euclid Street School, Swindon

Source: *The Euclidean* Summer 1941
www.highworthhistoricalsociety.co.uk
Headlandian Summer 1946, p.30

**COVEY
WALTER**
ROYAL NAVY (HMS Penelope)
- Stoker 1st class
- Died: 18.02.1944
- Brother of **WILLIAM COVEY** see below
- Attended Ferndale Road School, Swindon

Source: *North Wilts Herald* 10.03.1944, p.8 (photo)
Evening Advertiser 06.03.1944, p.1 (photo)

**COVEY
WILLIAM**
ROYAL AIR FORCE
- Flight Sergeant
- Died: 07.12.1941
- Brother of **WALTER COVEY** see above

Source: *North Wilts Herald* 10.03.1944, p.8 (photo)
Evening Advertiser 06.03.1944, p.1 (photo)

COWLEY
GEORGE FREDERICK
WILTSHIRE REGIMENT
- Private
- Age: 20
- Died: 21.05.1940
- Died at Dunkirk

Source:CWGC

COX
ROBERT GEORGE
ROYAL ARMY SERVICE CORPS
- Driver
- Age: 24
- Died: 01.06.1941

Source:CWGC

COX
STANLEY WALTER
ROYAL ENGINEERS
- Sapper
- Age: 33
- Died: 27.02.1943
- Attended Jennings Street School, Swindon

Source: *North Wilts Herald* 26.03.1943, p.8 (photo)
Evening Advertiser 24.03.1943, p.3 (photo)
Evening Advertiser 26.02.1944, p.2

COX
WILLIAM JOHN
ROYAL ENGINEERS
- Corporal
- Age: 24
- Died: 03.06.1941
- Buried in Chiseldon Cemetery

Source: *Evening Advertiser* 04.06.1945, p.8

CRANE
JACK ERIC
LANCASHIRE FUSILIERS
- Fusilier
- Age: 21
- Died: 16.10.1944

Source:CWGC

CREW
GEORGE ALFRED
MERCHANT NAVY (SS Toronto)
- Sailor
- Age: 18
- Died: 02.07.1941

Source:CWGC

CRITCHELY
RONALD JOHN
ROYAL AIR FORCE Voluntary Reserve
- Flight Sergeant

Source: The *Swindonian* Spring 1944, p.927

CROSS
GERALD CHARLES GEORGE
ROYAL AIR FORCE
- Aircraftman 2nd class
- Age: 18
- Died: 07.02.1942
- Attended Commonweal School, Swindon

Source: *Commonweal School Magazine* Summer 1942, p.3
North Wilts Herald 24.04.1942, p.3 (photo)
Evening Advertiser 23.04.1942, p.1 (photo)

CROSSLEY
RONALD JOHN
ROYAL AIR FORCE Voluntary Reserve
- Flight Sergeant (Navigator)
- Age: 25
- Died: 01.05.1943
- Attended Swindon Secondary School

Source: *North Wilts Herald* 12.11.1943, p.4 (photo)
www.highworthhistoricalsociety.co.uk
Evening Advertiser 09.11.1943, p.2
Highworth War Memorial

CUBBAGE (DFM)
BRION STANLEY
ROYAL AIR FORCE Voluntary Reserve
- Pilot Officer (Air Gunner)
- Died: 15.02.1944

Source: *North Wilts Herald* 12.12.1944, p.8;
North Wilts Herald 26.05.1944, p.5 (photo)
Evening Advertiser 11.12.1944, p.5
Evening Advertiser 22.05.1944, p.1 (photo)
See Awards and Medals

CULLINAN
THOMAS BRADY (TOMMY)
ROYAL ARTILLERY
- Gunner
- Age: 33
- Died: 11.04.1940
- Shot dead as result of an accident at an RAF station
- Grand National winning jockey
- Mother lived at the Lawn Lodge, Swindon
- Buried in Christ Church Cemetery, Swindon

Source: *Evening Advertiser* 12.04.2009, p.16

CURLEY
SIDNEY HOPKINS
MERCHANT NAVY
- Private
- Age: 20
- Died of wounds received while fire watching
- Attended Lethbridge Road School, Swindon

Source: *North Wilts Herald* 09.05.1941, p.5 (photo);

CUTTER
GEORGE
ROYAL AIR FORCE
Sergeant Air Gunner
- Age: 26
- Missing for 12 months, presumed dead July 1943

Source: "Build me an Ark', *Crossfire*, 1996 p.109
North Wilts Herald 09.07.1943, p.4
Evening Advertiser 02.07.1943, p.1 (photo)
Evening Advertiser 06.07.1945, p.2

D

DADGE
WILLIAM GEORGE HENRY
ROYAL AIR FORCE
- Sergeant Air Bomber
- Age: 22
- Died: 15.08.1943
- Part of a crew of bomber that went missing after attack on southern Italy
- Attended Clarence Street School, Swindon

Source: Swindon Scout Memorial
ww2talk.com
Evening Advertiser 25.08.1943, p.3 (photo)

DALY
WILLIAM JOHN
ROYAL AIR FORCE
- Rear Gunner
- Died: 18.07.1944

Source:CWGC
St Augustine War Memorial

DANCE
JAMES WILLIAM
Source: *'Build me an Ark'*, Crossfire, 1996, p.109

DAVIS
ILTED CHARLES JOHN
ROYAL NAVY (HMS Dorsetshire)
- Engineroom Artificer 4th class
- Age: 21
- Died: 05.04.1942
- Attended Wroughton School

Source:Wroughton War Memorial
Evening Advertiser 30.04.1942, p.1 (photo)
Wroughton History Group - Book 10 (2016), pp.75 & 102

DAVIS
JOHN DOUGLAS
ROYAL ARTILLERY 158 (Airborne) Field Regiment
- Gunner
- Age: 28
- Died: 14.05.1947

Source:CWGC

DAVIS
OWEN STANLEY (STAN)
ROYAL HORSE ARTILLERY
- Gunner
- Age: 23
- Died: 28.10.1942

Source: *North Wilts Herald* 20.11.1942, p.2
Great Western Railway Magazine January 1943, p.12
Evening Advertiser 18.11.1942, p.2 (photo)

DAVIS
WILLIAM CHARLES
ROYAL NAVY (HMS Beagle)
- Able Seaman
- Age: 55
- Died: 01.01.1940
- Buried in Whitworth Road Cemetery, Swindon

Source:CWGC

DAY
VICTOR JESSE
ROYAL ARMY SERVICE CORPS
- Driver
- Age: 30
- Died: 04.04.1943
- Attended Clarence Street School, Swindon

Source: *Evening Advertiser* 12.04.1943, p.4 (photo)
Evening Advertiser 04.04.1944, p.8

DAY (BEM MiD OBE) SIDNEY FRANK
ROYAL NAVY (HMS Wyvern)
- Petty Officer Stoker
- Age: 35
- Died: 22.02.1943

Source: St. Augustine Church Memorial
North Wilts Herald 05.03.1943, p.5 (photo)
North Wilts Herald 09.07.1943, p.8 (photo)
Evening Advertiser 27.02.1943, p.5 (photo)
Evening Advertiser 07.07.1943, p.4 (photo) lists citation for Mention in Despatches
See Awards and Medals

DEACON BERTRAM FRANK
ROYAL NAVY (HM Sub Odin)
- Chief Engineroom Artificer
- Age: 37
- Died: 27.06.1940

Source: CWGC

DEMPSTER JOHN BARLOW
ROYAL MARINES
- Marine
- Died: 08.07.1946

Source: CWGC

DENTON ROBERT KENNETH (BOB)
ROYAL NAVY (HMS Glorious)
- Able Seaman
- Age: 23
- Died: 08.06.1940
- Killed when HMS Glorious was sunk

Source: *Evening Advertiser* 30.7.1940, p.2 (photo)

DE VEER HENDRICK
Source: Swindon High School plaque in Christ Church, Swindon

DICKENSON KENNETH
ROYAL AIR FORCE Voluntary Reserve
- Flight Engineer
- Age: 21
- Died: 22.05.1944
- Son of ex STFC captain Wally Dickenson

Source: *Evening Advertiser* 23.05.1944, p.5 (photo), reported missing
Evening Advertiser 03.08.1944, p.2 (photo)
Evening Advertiser 21.05.1945, p.2
North Wilts Herald 02.06.1944, p.5 (photo)
North Wilts Herald 04.08.1944, p.3 (photo)

DIXON ALFRED JAMES
GLOUCESTER REGIMENT
- Private
- Age: 23
- Died: 13.02.1945

Source: CWGC

DORE JOSEPH LAWSON
ROYAL NAVY (HMS Fieldfare)
- Air Fitter
- Age: 40
- Died: 11.11.1945

Source: CWGC

DOWDESWELL RAMSEY DONALD (DON)
ROYAL NAVY (HMS Collingwood)
- Ordinary Seaman
- Age: 18
- Died: 18.06.1943
- A sleeping hut at HMS Collingwood, Hampshire was hit by a bomb, killing 33 men, most aged 17-18

Source:*Evening Advertiser* 19.06.1945, p.2
Swindon Scout Memorial

DOWSE CONDOR CHARLES
ROYAL AIR FORCE
- Sergeant Air Gunner
- Age: 22
- Died: 09.08.1944

Source: *Evening Advertiser* 09.08.1945, p.2

DRAPER HUBERT FRANK
WILTSHIRE REGIMENT
- Corporal
- Age: 30
- Died: 28.01.1944
- Had been evacuated from Dunkirk
- Killed when the train taking him to a prison camp in Germany was bombed in Italy

Source:*North Wilts Herald* 01.12.1944, p.3 (photo)
Evening Advertiser 30.11.1944, p.2 (photo)

DUGAIT JOHN MARCEL
ROYAL ARMY SERVICE CORPS
- Driver
- Age: 27
- Died: 22.12.1942
- Buried in Lower Stratton Cemetery

Source:CWGC

DUNN FREDERICK
ROYAL AIR FORCE
- Sergeant (Air bomber)
- Age: 22
- Died: 22.11.1943
- Attended Cirencester Grammar School

Source: *North Wilts Herald* 03.12.1943, p.2 (photo)
Evening Advertiser 03.12.1943, p.5 (photo)

DURNELL (BEM) CLARENCE WILLIAM
ROYAL NAVY
- Engineroom Artificer
- Age: 20
- Died: 25.02.1942
- GWR Magazine spells surname Durnall

Source: *Great Western Railway Magazine* November 1942, p.197
Stratton Green Baptist Church memorial
www.highworthhistoricalsociety.co.uk
See Awards and Medals

E

EARTHRIDGE
FREDERICK JOHN
WILTSHIRE REGIMENT
- Sergeant
- Age: 30
- Died: 06.08.1944
- Attended Sanford Street School, Swindon

North Wilts Herald 25.08.1944, p.5 (photo)
Evening Advertiser 21.08.1944, p.1 (photo)
Evening Advertiser 02.08.1945, p.2

EDDOLLS
ERIC EDWARD
ROYAL ARTILLERY
- Gunner
- Died: Between 26-27.04.1941

Source: www.highworthhistoricalsociety.co.uk

EDGINGTON
DAVID WILLIAM
ROYAL ARTILLERY
- Gunner
- Age: 26
- Died: 03.09.1945

Source: *Great Western Railway Magazine* November 1945, p.183

EDMEADS
ANTHONY CHARLES HENRY
ROYAL AIR FORCE Voluntary Reserve
- Sergeant Air Gunner
- Age: 22
- Died: 02.09.1940

Source: CWGC

EDMONDS
ANTHONY RAY
ROYAL NAVY (HMS Hood)
- Writer
- Age: 20
- Died: 24.05.1941
- Attended Commonweal School

Source: CWGC

EDMUNDS
F. E.
AUSTRALIAN FORCES
- Corporal
- Born in Swindon, moved to Australia aged 15
- Possibly Frederick Ellis Edmonds (AIF) died 02.05.41 aged 28 (CWGC)

Source: *North Wilts Herald* 15.08.1941, p.3

EDWARDS
ALBERT HENRY
ROYAL ARMY SERVICE CORPS
- Driver
- Age: 29
- Died: 17.06.1940
- Drowned on the RMS Lancastria

Source: *North Wilts Herald* 23.05.1941, p.5

ELMS
WILLIAM GEORGE (BILLY)
ROYAL ARMOURED CORPS
- Trooper
- Age: 21
- Died: 20.01.1945

Source: Wroughton War Memorial
Evening Advertiser 06.02.1945, p5
Wroughton History Group - Book 10 (2016), p.75

ELY
PETER OLIVER WILLIAM
- PARACHUTE REGIMENT
- Private
- Age: 19
- Died: 10.08.1944

Source: Highworth War Memorial Highworth Link November 2011, pp.4-5) www.highworthhistoricalsociety.co.uk

EMBLING
J.
Source: Hook War Memorial

ETHERINGTON
HARRY MARK
ROYAL AIR FORCE Voluntary Reserve
- Flying Officer/Air Bomber
- Age: 28
- Died: 11.08.1943

Source: CWGC

EVANS
VICTOR ERNEST JAMES
ROYAL ARMY ORDNANCE CORPS
- Private
- Age: 25
- Died: 31.03.1941
- Died and buried in Sierra Leone

Source: CWGC

EVANS
WILLIAM EDWARD HASLEWOOD
ROYAL NAVY (submarine Sterlet)
- Engineroom Artificer 3rd class
- Age: 26
- Died: 27.04.1940
- Reported missing when Sterlet was lost south of Narvik.
- Believed struck by anti-submarine trawler 18.4.1944
- Attended Westcott Place School, Swindon

Source: *North Wilts Herald* 03.05.1940, p.7
Evening Advertiser 02.05.1940, p.1 (photo),
swindonatwar.blogspot.com/30.01.12

F

FARMELO
WILLIAM
ROYAL INNISKILLING
FUSILIERS
- Fusilier
- Age: 23
- Died: 16.05.1944
- Parents came from Purton

Source: CWGC

FARRIER (MiD)
ERNEST CHARLES
ROYAL NAVY (HMS Niger)
- Petty Officer Stoker
- Died: 06.07.1942

Source: CWGC
See Awards and Medals

FARTHING
MARJORIE EILEEN ETHEL
QUEEN ALEXANDRA'S
IMPERIAL NURSING SERVICE
- Sister
- Age: 31
- Died: 02.12.1945

Source: CWGC

FEAR
FREDERICK ROWLAND
PARACHUTE REGIMENT AAC
- Corporal
- Died: 13.12.1944

Source: *Great Western Railway Magazine* February 1945, p.32

FELL
ERNEST
LINCOLNSHIRE REGIMENT
- Sergeant
- Age: 33
- Died: 27.06.1944

Source: *North Wilts Herald* 28.07.1944, p.5 (photo)
Evening Advertiser 25.07.1944, p.4 (photo)
Evening Advertiser 27.06.1945, p.2

FERGUSON
IAN (JOHN) WOODMAN
ROYAL AIR FORCE Voluntary Reserve
- Sergeant (Navigator)
- Age: 20
- Died: 26.09.1943
- Attended Commonweal School, Swindon

Source: *Commonweal School Magazine* Summer 1944, p.5
Great Western Railway Magazine January 1944, p.16,
North Wilts Herald 01.10.1943, p.4 (photo)
Evening Advertiser 29.09.1943, p.8 (photo)

FISHER
FREDERICK WILLIAM
ROYAL ARTILLERY
- Gunner
- Age: 28
- Died: 14.09.1941

Source: Lydiard Millicent War Memorial

FISHER
R.
- Possibly Reginald Fisher, Private 14736630 Devonshire Regiment

Source: Hook War Memorial

FLEWELLING
EWART
YORK AND LANCASTER REGIMENT
- Private
- Died: 11.10.1943
- Wife lived in Purton

Source: CWGC

FOOTE
HUBERT
ROYAL NAVY (HMS Galatea)
- Leading Steward
- Died: 15.12.1941

Source: *Evening Advertiser* 15.12.1944, p.2
Evening Advertiser 30.12.1943, p.2

FORD-DEACON
LEONARD
VETERAN'S GUARD OF CANADA
- Private
- Age: 57

Died: 02.02.1945
Source: CWGC

FORKIN
MICHAEL JOSEPH (JOSEPH)
LANCASHIRE FUSILIERS
- Fusilier
- Age: 34
- Died: 16.10.1944

Source: *Evening Advertiser* 01.11.1944, p.2

FORSTER
M.
ROYAL NAVY
- Engineroom Artificer

Source: *Great Western Railway Magazine* March 1945, p.48

FOSTER
LEONARD FREDERICK
ROYAL AIR FORCE
- Aircraftsman 2nd class/ Wireless Operator
- Age: 32
- Died: 05.04.1940

Source: CWGC

FOWLER
ALAN
DORSET REGIMENT
- Sergeant
- Age: 37
- Died: 10.07.1944
- *North Wilts Herald* says aged 32
- Played for Swindon Town Football Club

Source: *North Wilts Herald* 25.08.1944, p.5 (photo)
Evening Advertiser 21.08.1944, p.5 (photo)
Evening Advertiser 26.08.1944, p.3 (photo)
Evening Advertiser 10.07.1945, p.2

FOX
EDWARD
HAMPSHIRE REGIMENT
- Private
- Age: 40
- Died: 21.04.1944
- Died of meningitis at Burden Neurological Institute, Stoke Gifford
- Buried in Broad Hinton Cemetery

Source: *Wroughton History Group - Book 10* (2016), p.75

FRANCIS
CLAUDE
ROYAL NAVY (HMS Sub Perseus)
- Engineroom Artificer 4th Class
- Age: 24
- Died: 19.12.1941

Source: CWGC

FRANKLIN
HERBERT JOHN
- Private

Source: *Evening Advertiser* 22.07.1940, p.4

FREEMAN
WILLIAM THOMAS
ROYAL AIR FORCE Voluntary Reserve
- Sergeant
- Age: 25
- Died: 21.04.1944

Source: CWGC

FULLER
ERIC NORMAN
ROYAL ARTILLERY 39 Battery 14 Light Anti Aircraft Regiment
- Gunner/Lance Bombardier
- Age: 19
- Died: 31.07.1941
- Died of wounds received in Egypt
- From Church Road, Liddington

Source: *Great Western Railway Magazine* December 1941, p.328
Plaque in STEAM, Swindon

FULLER
GERALD SYDNEY
ROYAL AIR FORCE
- Corporal
- Age: 22
- Died: 05.07.1942

Source: CWGC

G

GADD
JOHN
Source: Bishopstone War Memorial

GALBRAITH
IVOR SCARLETT CAMPBELL
ROYAL AIR FORCE Voluntary Reserve
Flying Officer (Pilot)
- Age: 24
- Died: 05.01.1943
- Buried in Wroughton Cemetery

Source: www.roll-of-honour.com/wiltshire/wroughton

GALE
SAMUEL ARTHUR CHARLES
PIONEER CORPS
- Private
- Age: 26
- Died: 24.11.1940
- Buried in Whitworth Road Cemetery, Swindon

Source: *Evening Advertiser* 02.12.1940, p.4 (photo)

GANTLETT
ALBERT
QUEEN'S OWN ROYAL WEST KENT REGIMENT
- Lance Corporal
- Died: 24.10.1944
- Attended Swindon High School, Swindon

Source: Swindon High School Memorial in Christ Church, Swindon

GARDNER
LESLIE CHARLES
ROYAL ELECTRICAL AND MECHANICAL ENGINEERS
- Staff Sergeant
- Age: 30
- Died: 01.02.1946

Source: CWGC

GARRAWAY
SIDNEY FRANK
ROYAL AIR FORCE Voluntary Reserve
- Aircraftman 2nd class
- Age: 27
- Died: 14.11.1940
- Buried in Christ Church Cemetery, Swindon
- Killed during an air raid

Source: *Great Western Railway Magazine* January 1941, p.25
North Wilts Herald 22.11.1940, p.3 (photo);
Evening Advertiser 19.11.1940, p.2 (photo);
Evening Advertiser 21.08.1941, p.1

GATEHOUSE
THOMAS HENRY
OXFORDSHIRE AND BUCKINGHAMSHIRE LIGHT INFANTRY
- Private
- Age: 29
- Died: 26.11.1941

Source: CWGC

GAUNTLETT
MAURICE LOWDEN
ROYAL AIR FORCE Voluntary Reserve
- Pilot Officer/Air Gunner
- Age: 34
- Died: 07.11.1940

Source:*North Wilts Herald* 15.11.1940, p.4 (photo)
North Wilts Herald 22.11.1940, p.5
Evening Advertiser 09.11.1940, p.1 (photo)
Evening Advertiser 12.11.1940, p.5

GEE
JAMES
ROYAL ARTILLERY
- Gunner
- Age: 39
- Died: 28.01.1940
- Killed by a train

Source:*Evening Advertiser* 01.02.1940, p3 (photo)

GIBBON
JOHN
ROYAL WELCH FUSILIERS
Sergeant
- Age: 37
- Died: 23.05.1940

Source: CWGC

GIBBS
ROBERT WILLIAM
HOME GUARD
- Civilian
- Age: 33
- Died: 31.08.1942
- Died in Victoria Hospital, Swindon

Source:CWGC

GIBBS
RONALD WILLIAM
ROYAL AIR FORCE
- Sergeant Pilot
- Age: 22
- Died: 30.08.1944
- Listed on Wills factory plaque in St Luke's Church, Swindon
- Attended Clarence Street School, Swindon

Source: *Evening Advertiser* 07.09.1944, p.1 (photo)
Wills Works Magazine August 1945, p.16
Wills Works Magazine March 1946, p.13

GIBBS
STANLEY REGINALD JAMES
ROYAL ARTILLERY
- Gunner
- Age: 22
- Died: 05.08.1944
- Attended Pinehurst School, Swindon

Source:*North Wilts Herald* 22.09.1944, p.4
Evening Advertiser 25.08.1944, p.1 (photo)

GIBSON
ARTHUR
THE GREEN HOWARDS
(YORKSHIRE REGIMENT)
- Lance Corporal
- Age: 29
- Died: 17.10.1944
- Evacuated at Dunkirk
- Attended Swindon High School, Swindon

Source:*North Wilts Herald* 03.11.1944, p.4 (photo)
Evening Advertiser 27.10.1944, pp.2/4
Christ Church War Memorial, Swindon

GILDER
CECIL (FREDERICK)
ROYAL AIR FORCE
- Sergeant/Air Gunner
- Age: 22
- Died: 20.12.1942
- CWGC lists him as Frederick
- Attended The College, Victoria Road, Swindon

Source:*North Wilts Herald* 09.04.1943, p.5 (photo)
Evening Advertiser 03.04.1943, p.8 (photo)

GILLIGAN (MM)
FREDERICK JOHN
ROYAL INNISKILLING FUSILIERS
- Sergeant
- Age: 34
- Died: 01.10.1945

Source:*Evening Advertiser* 10.11.1945, p.6
See Awards and Medals

GLASS
WILLIAM ERNEST
HOME GUARD
- Civilian
- Age: 27
- Died: 05.05.1942
- Son of William George and Florence Annie Glass, of 354 Cheney Manor Road, Swindon
- Died at Victoria Road, Swindon

Source:CWGC

GLEED
HARRY
- Possibly **ALBERT HENRY GLEED** below

Source: Wanborough War Memorial

GLEED
ALBERT HENRY
SOMESET LIGHT INFANTRY
- Private
- Age: 27
- Died: 29.06.1944
- Son of Albert and Ada Gleed of Wanborough
- Possibly same man as **HARRY GLEED** above

Source: CWGC

GOUGH
ERIC WILLIAM
ROYAL ARMY ORDNANCE CORPS
- Private
- Age: 27
- Died: 12.10.1943

Source:Lydiard Millicent War Memorial
see Prisoners of War

GOUGH
HERBERT WILLIAM
ROYAL ARTILLERY/ACC
- Lance Corporal
- Age: 21
- Died: 10.09.1944
- Attended Even Swindon School, Swindon

Source: *Great Western Railway Magazine* December 1944, p.192
St Augustine Church Memorial
North Wilts Herald 17.11.1944, p.5 (photo)
Evening Advertiser 11.11.1944, p.8 (photo)

GOUGH
REGINALD LESLIE
ROYAL ENGINEERS
- Sapper
- Age: 26
- Died: 29.09.1941
- Attended Rodbourne Cheney School, Swindon

Source: *North Wilts Herald* 10.10.1941, p.5

GOWEN
HARRY GEORGE
WILTSHIRE REGIMENT
- Private
- Age: 24
- Died: 28.05.1942
- Family sources say died on board ship en route to Madagascar

Source: 'Build me an Ark', *Crossfire*, 1996 p.109
North Wilts Herald 12.06.1942, p.8 (photo)

GRAHAM
EDWIN CYRIL
ROYAL AIR FORCE
- Wireless Operator/Air Gunner
- Age: 26
- Died: 15.07.1941
- Buried in Christ Church Cemetery, Swindon

Source: CWGC

GRAY
DOUGLAS JOHN
ROYAL NAVY (HMS Itchen)
- Ordinary Seaman
- Age: 21
- Died: 23.09.1943
- Son of Alfred J Gray, ex President of Swindon Chamber of Commerce and Swindon Rotary Club
- Killed when HMS Itchen was torpedoed
- Attended Swindon High School, Swindon

Source: *North Wilts Herald* 01.10.1943, p.8
Christ Church War Memorial, Swindon
Evening Advertiser 29.09.1943, p.3
Swindon Scout Memorial
ww2talk.com

GREEN
GEORGE FRANCIS ROWLAND
ROYAL AIR FORCE Voluntary Reserve
- Flying Officer
- Died: 26.11.1943

Source: *Great Western Railway Magazine* September 1944, p.143
St. Augustine Church Memorial

GREENMAN
WILFRED JAMES
ROYAL AIR FORCE Voluntary Reserve
- Aircraftman 2nd class
- Age: 20
- Died: 17.06.1940

Source: *Great Western Railway Magazine* January 1945, p.15
Evening Advertiser 25.06.1940, p.1
Evening Advertiser 21.06.2010, p.18
Evening Advertiser 16.06.1945, p.2

GREENWOOD
WILLIAM LUKE
ROYAL AIR FORCE Voluntary Reserve
- Leading Aircraftman
- Age: 43
- Died: 09.06.1945
- Buried in Christ Church Cemetery, Swindon

Source: CWGC

GREGORY
PETER M.
ROYAL AIR FORCE
- Aircraftman
- Attended Swindon High School, Swindon

Source: *Great Western Railway Magazine* May 1941, p.137
Evening Advertiser 01.03.1941, p.2
Christ Church War Memorial, Swindon

GRIFFIN
RONALD FREDERICK GEORGE
ROYAL AIR FORCE
- Leading Aircraftman
- Age: 19
- Died: 29.11.1941
- Buried in Christ Church Cemetery, Swindon
- Attended Swindon Secondary School

Source: *Swindonian* Autumn 1941, p.886
Great Western Railway Magazine March 1942, p.65
Headlandian Summer 1946, p.30

GRIFFIN
ROYSTON
FLEET AIR ARM (HMS Grebe)
- Sub-Lieutenant
- Died: 28.12.1941
- Left Swindon as a child. Uncle and Aunt lived at Carr Street
- Killed in aerial combat near Tobruk

Source: *Evening Advertiser* 12.03.1942, p.1 (photo)
Evening Advertiser 28.12.1943, p.2

GRIGGS
LESLIE CHARLES
ROYAL NAVY (HMS Beverley)
- Stoker
- Age: 25
- Died: 11.04.1943
- Survived sinking of Ark Royal, missing presumed killed after sinking of HMS Beverley
- Attended Sanford Street School, Swindon

Source: *North Wilts Herald* 07.05.1943, p.5 (photo)
Evening Advertiser 04.05.1943, p.5 (photo)
Evening Advertiser 11.04.1944, p.2

GRIST
ALBERT WILLIAM GEORGE (BERT)
WILTSHIRE REGIMENT
- Corporal
- Age: 27
- Died: 22.07.1944
- Attended Gorse Hill School, Swindon

Source: *North Wilts Herald* 18.08.1944, p.5 (photo)
Evening Advertiser 12.08.1944, p.2 (photo)
Evening Advertiser 23.07.1945, p.2
Evening Advertiser 24.07.1945, p.2

GWILLIM
LESLIE PERCY
ROYAL AIR FORCE Voluntary Reserve
- Leading Aircraftman
- Age: 21
- Died: 19.05.1944
- Buried in Radnor Street Cemetery, Swindon

Source: *Evening Advertiser* 19.05.1945, p.2

H

HACKER
GORDON MAYO
ROYAL AIR FORCE Voluntary Reserve
- Sergeant Navigator
- Age: 22
- Died: 29.06.1943
- Attended Euclid Street School, Swindon

Source: *The Euclidean* Summer 1944
Headlandian Summer 1946, p.30

HACKER
RONALD ARTHUR
SOUTH WALES BORDERERS
- Private
- Age: 25
- Died: 15.11.1944

Source: *North Wilts Herald* 15.12.1944, p.4 (photo)
Evening Advertiser 13.12.1944, p.2

HAINES
GEORGE FRANK
ROYAL ENGINEERS
- Sergeant
- Age: 24
- Died: 02.03.1943

Source: *Great Western Railway Magazine* May 1943, p.76

HALL
PATRICK ANTHONY
ROYAL AIR FORCE
- Pilot Officer
- Attended Swindon High School, Swindon

Source: Swindon High School Memorial in Christ Church, Swindon
Swindon Scout Memorial in Scout HQ, Swindon

HALL
RONALD FREDERICK H.
5th WILTSHIRE REGIMENT
- Private
- Age: 24
- Died: 10.07.1944
- Reburied next to lifelong friend **W.J. HAWKINS** (see below) in Bayeux British Cemetery
- Attended Euclid Street School, Swindon

Source: *Great Western Railway Magazine* September 1944, p.143
North Wilts Herald 22.06.1945, p.3
North Wilts Herald 04.08.1944, p.3 (photo)
Evening Advertiser 02.08.1944, pp.2/5 (photo)
Evening Advertiser 21.06.1945, p.6
Evening Advertiser 10.07.1945, p.2

HAMLEY
TERENCE EDWARD
ROYAL AIR FORCE Voluntary Reserve
- Sergeant
- Age: 21
- Died: 9.05.1943
- Attended Commonweal School, Swindon

Source: *Commonweal School Magazine* Summer 1943, pp.5-6
Commonweal School Magazine Summer 1944, p.5
North Wilts Herald 21.05.1943, p.5 (photo)
Evening Advertiser 09.05.1944, p.2

HAMSON
DOUGLAS CHARLES
ROYAL AIR FORCE Voluntary Reserve
Leading Aircraftman
- Age: 22
- Died: 13.06.1945
- Buried in Wroughton cemetery

Source: www.roll-of-honour.com/wiltshire/wroughton

HARBERT
HARRY GEORGE
ROYAL NAVY (HMS Sub Thames)
- Able Seaman
- Age: 32
- Died: 03.08.1940

Source: CWGC

HARFIELD
FREDERICK GEORGE
ROYAL AIR FORCE Voluntary Reserve
- Leading Aircraftman
- Age: 32
- Died: 02.04.1946
- Buried in Radnor Street Cemetery, Swindon

Source: CWGC

HARMAN
FRANCIS WILFRED
ROYAL AIR FORCE Voluntary Reserve
- Wireless Operator/Air Gunner
- Age: 22
- Died: 22.12.1945
- Brother of **ROLAND CLIFFORD HARMAN** (below)

Source: CWGC

HARMAN
FRANK ANGEL
ROYAL TANK REGIMENT
- Trooper
- Age: 30
- Died: 25.09.1944
- all 10 of Mrs Harman's sons were in the forces

Source: *North Wilts Herald* 13.10.1944, p.4 (photo)

HARMAN
ROLAND CLIFFORD
FLEET AIR ARM
- Died at home in Swindon on 28.06.1945, six months after being invalided out of the Fleet Air Arm of the Royal Navy
- He was at HMS Royal Arthur in 1941, Class A33
- Brother of **FRANCIS HARMAN** (above)

Source: http://archive.is/oNtus

HARRIS
DONALD REUBEN
ROYAL AIR FORCE Voluntary Reserve
- Sergeant
- Age: 21
- Died: 12.09.1941
- Reported missing Sept 1941 following bombing raid over Germany, presumed killed March 1942
- Worked as a clerk in the *Evening Advertiser* office

Source: 'In Memoriam,' 1946, Swindon Press (photo)
North Wilts Herald 20.03.1942, p.8 (photo)
Evening Advertiser 17.09.1941, p.2 (photo)

HARRIS
JOHN FREDERICK
ROYAL AIR FORCE Voluntary Reserve
- Flying Officer
- Age: 29
- Died: 29.03.1943

Source: CWGC

HARRISON
STANLEY
WILTSHIRE REGIMENT
- Corporal
- Age: 38
- Died: 19.07.1945
- Buried in Whitworth Road Cemetery, Swindon

Source: CWGC

HART
HENRY ROBERT (HARRY)
ROYAL HORSE GUARDS
- Corporal
- Age: 22
- Died: 27.09.1944

Source: *Great Western Railway Magazine* December 1944, p.192
15 Shop Memorial, STEAM, Swindon
North Wilts Herald 13.10.1944, p.4 (photo)
Evening Advertiser 06.10.44, p.5 (photo)

HARWOOD
ROYSTON HUBERT
ROYAL AIR FORCE Voluntary Reserve
- Leading Aircraftman
- Age: 23
- Died: 24.07.1944
- Killed in an aircraft accident
- Buried in Radnor Street Cemetery, Swindon

Source: *Evening Advertiser* 24.07.1944, p.2

HAWKES
LEONARD HERBERT
ROYAL IRISH FUSILIERS
- Fusilier
- Age: 27
- Died: 31.03.1944
- Died at Monte Cassino

Source: CWGC

HAWKINS
WILLIAM CHARLES (BILL)
WILTSHIRE REGIMENT
- Sergeant
- Age: 25
- Died: 10.07.1944
- Reburied next to lifelong friend **R.F. HALL** (see above) in Bayeux British Cemetery
- Attended Euclid Street School, Swindon

Source: St Augustine Church Memorial
North Wilts Herald 22.06.1945, p.3
North Wilts Herald 04.08.1944, p.3 (photo)
Evening Advertiser 31.07.1944 pp.2/5 (photo)
Evening Advertiser 21.06.1945, p.6
Headlandian Summer 1946, p.30

HAYES
ALBERT/ALFRED EDWARD
ROYAL AIR FORCE
- Sergeant Flight Engineer
- Age: 39
- Died: 12.06.1943
- *Evening Advertiser* lists him as Alfred
- Attended Sanford Street School, Swindon

Source:*North Wilts Herald* 03.09.43, p.8 (photo)
Evening Advertiser 31.08.43, p.1

HAYNES
GEOFFREY
ROYAL AIR FORCE Voluntary Reserve
- Flight Sergeant
- Age: 23
- Died: 25.02.1944

Source: CWGC

HAYNES
RICHARD ANTHONY
ROYAL ARTILLERY
- Gunner
- Age: 18
- Died: 25.08.1940
- Died on despatch riding duty in southern England
- Attended Swindon High School, Swindon
- Buried in Whitworth Road Cemetery, Swindon

Source: *North Wilts Herald* 30.08.1940, p.5 (photo);
Christ Church War Memorial, Swindon
Evening Advertiser 23.08.10, p.16
Evening Advertiser 29.08.1940, p.4
Swindon Scout Memorial
ww2talk.com

HAZEL
GEORGE OLIVER
ROYAL ARTILLERY
- Gunner
- Age: 40
- Died: 11.07.1945

Source:CWGC

HAZELL
HAROLD WILFRED
ROYAL AIR FORCE
- Sergeant
- Age: 46
- Died: 12.08.1942
- Served with Royal Flying Corps in World War One

Source: *Great Western Railway Magazine* November 1942, p.196
15 Shop Memorial, STEAM, Swindon

HEAD
EDWARD ALBERT (TED)
ROYAL NAVY (HMS Tonbridge)
- Engine room Artificer
- Age: 26
- Died: 22.08.1941

Source:*Evening Advertiser* 25.03.2010, p.16
Evening Advertiser 02.09.1941 p.2 (photo)

HEAD
STANLEY ERNEST
DUKE OF WELLINGTON LIGHT INFANTRY
- Private
- Age: 18
- Died: 29.10.1944

Source:Highworth War Memorial
Highworth Link November 2011, pp.4-5
www.highworthhistoricalsociety.co.uk

HEAVENS (MiD) ROBERT ERIC
SAS REGIMENT AAC
- Sergeant
- Age: 41
- Died: 07.07.1944
- Shot while a Prisoner of War
- Attended Clarence Street School, Swindon

Source: *Great Western Railway Magazine* October 1944 p.160
Great Western Railway Magazine August 1945, p.133
North Wilts Herald 06.07.1945, p.5 (photo)
Evening Advertiser 15.08.1944, p.5 (photo)
Evening Advertiser 29.06.1945, p.2 (photo)
See Awards and Medals

HENLY ROBERT WILLIAM
ROYAL AIR FORCE Voluntary Reserve
- Pilot Officer
- Age: 20
- Died: 21.12.1942
- Reported missing 21.12.1942, in May 1943, Red Cross notified parents that all 7 occupants of aircraft had been killed on raid on Munich 21.12.1942
- Attended Sanford Street School, Swindon

Source: *North Wilts Herald* 01.01.1943, p.4 (photo)
North Wilts Herald 14.05.1943, p.4 (photo)
Evening Advertiser 21.12.1944, p.2
Evening Advertiser 11.05.1943, p.3 (photo)
Evening Advertiser 21.12.1943, p.2
Scouts Roll of Honour
ww2talk.com

HERBERT GORDON RICHARD EDWARD
ROYAL NAVY (HMS Drake)
- Artificer
- Age: 22
- Died: 22.07.1946
- Buried in Whitworth Road Cemetery, Swindon

Source:*Great Western Railway Magazine* October 1946, p.228

HESLOP
JOHN WILLIAM
ROYAL NAVY (HMS Glorious)
- Able Seaman
- Age: 38
- Died: 08.06.1940

Source: CWGC

HICKS
FRANCIS LESLIE
ROYAL AUSTRALIAN AIR FORCE
- Flight Sergeant
- Age: 30
- Died: 19.02.1943
- Died when plane crashed on while on exercise
- Buried in Wroughton Cemetery

Source: www.roll-of-honour.com/wiltshire/wroughton
Wroughton History Group - Book 10 (2016), p.109

HIGGINS
CYRIL
WILTSHIRE REGIMENT
- Lance Corporal
- Age: 30
- Died: 10.07.1944
- Played for Swindon Town Reserves

Source: *North Wilts Herald* 04.08.1944, p.3
Evening Advertiser 29.07.1944, p.2
Evening Advertiser 04.08.1944, p.5 (photo)
Evening Advertiser 10.07.1945, p.2
Evening Advertiser 14.07.1945, p.2

HIGGINSON
HARRY
ROYAL AIR FORCE
- Flight Sergeant
- Age: 27
- Died: 26.10.1941
- Attended Swindon Secondary School, Swindon

Source: *North Wilts Herald* 31.10.1941, p.2 (photo)
Evening Advertiser 27.10.1941, p.1 (photo)

HILL
ERIC ALBERT
ROYAL ARMOURED CORPS
- Trooper
- Age: 21
- Died: 10.10.1941
- Buried in Whitworth Road Cemetery, Swindon

Source: CWGC

HILL
HENRY
- Perhaps same man as Henry John Cawardine Hill below

Source: "Build me an Ark', *Crossfire*, 1996, p.109

HILL
HENRY JOHN CAWARDINE
INDIAN ARMY ORDNANCE CORPS
- Major
- Age: 33
- Died: 26.07.1943
- Perhaps same man as Henry Hill above

Source: CWGC

HILL
J.
ROYAL NAVY
- Engine room artificer

Source:*Great Western Railway Magazine* November 1942, p.196

HILL
JACK ALFRED
ROYAL MARINES (HMS Sultan)
- Marine
- Age: 27
- Died: 09.08.1945

Source:CWGC

HILL
RALPH JOHN
Source: St Barnabas memorial plaque, St Barnabas Church, Swindon

HISCOCKS
THOMAS JOHN RICHARD (CHARLIE)
ROYAL SUSSEX REGIMENT
- Corporal
- Age: 22
- Died: 01.11.1945
- Died in India of meningitis
- Buried in Wroughton Cemetery

Wroughton History Group - Book 10 (2016), p.76
Evening Advertiser 10.11.1945, p.6

HOBBS
FRANK
ROYAL AIR FORCE Voluntary Reserve Flight Sergeant/Air Gunner
- Age: 21
- Died: 31.03.1944
- 51 Squadron, Operation Nurnberg. Took off at 22:17 from RAF Snaith. Homebound, believed to have been hit by flak and at Bietigheim, 18 km NNW of Stuttgart.

Source:CWGC

HOBBS
FREDERICK CHARLES
WILTSHIRE REGIMENT
- Private
- Age: 29
- Died: 23.05.1940

Source:CWGC

HODDELL
ROY COPE
ROYAL AIR FORCE
- Leading Aircraftman
- Age: 19
- Died: 23.07.1941

Source:CWGC

HODDINOTT
DONALD JOHN
ROYAL AIR FORCE Voluntary Reserve
- Flight Sergeant/Air Gunner
- Age: 31
- Died: 06.04.1944
- Parents lived in Fairford

Source:Blunsdon War Memorial

**HODGES
JOHN HENRY**
ROYAL ARTILLERY
- Lance bombardier
- Age: 24
- Died: 08.09.1944

Source: CWGC

**HOGARTH
PETER**
ROYAL AIR FORCE
- Pilot Officer
- Age: 26
- Died: 13.04.1941
- Killed in Greece

Source: *Evening Advertiser* 23.04.1941, p.1 (photo)

**HOLE
ALFRED**
ROYAL NAVY (HMS Avenger)
- Able Seaman
- Died: 15.11.1942

www.royalmailmemorials.com/memorial/swindon-postal-district-war-memorial

**HOLLICK
FREDERICK WILLIAM**
ROYAL AIR FORCE Voluntary Reserve
- Aircraftsman 1st Class
- Age: 29
- Died: 22.11.1942
- Buried at Rodbourne Cheney Cemetery

Source: CWGC

**HOLLICK
WILFRED (PETER)**
ROYAL AIR FORCE
- Flight Sergeant
- Died: 20.06.1943
- Attended Commonweal School, Swindon

Source: *Great Western Railway Magazine* August 1943, p.125, St Augustine Church Memorial 15 Shop Memorial, STEAM, Swindon
Evening Advertiser 20.06.1945, p.2

**HOLLISTER
WILLIAM FREDERICK GEORGE**
ROYAL AIR FORCE
- Age: 29
- Died: 20.06.1940

Source: St Augustine Church Memorial, Swindon

**HOLLOWAY
CHARLES HENRY**
WILTSHIRE REGIMENT
- Private
- Age: 22
- Died: 26.08.1944

Source: CWGC

HOLLOWAY
FREDERICK MARILLIER
ROYAL ARMY ORDNANCE CORPS
- Captain
- Died of 'sleeping sickness' in British Military Hospital Rawalpindi
- Attended Swindon High School, Swindon
- CWGC states Indian Electrical & Mechanical Engineers

Source: *Great Western Railway Magazine* July 1945, p.116
North Wilts Herald 20.04.1945, p.3 (photo)
North Wilts Herald 13.07.1945, p.4
Christ Church War Memorial, Swindon
Evening Advertiser 11.07.1945, p.2
Swindon Scout Memorial

HONEYMAN
GEORGE WILLIAM
ROYAL ENGINEERS
- Corporal
- Age: 39
- Died: 07.09.1946
- Buried in Whitworth Road Cemetery, Swindon

Source: CWGC

HOPKINS
SIDNEY
CHESHIRE REGIMENT
- Private
- Age: 21
- Died: 04.05.1941
- Buried in Christ Church Cemetery, Swindon

Source: CWGC

HORTON
ARTHUR HERBERT JAMES
WILTSHIRE REGIMENT
- Private
- Age: 21
- Died: 10.07.1944
- Married 6 days before embarking for D Day
- Attended Kingsdown School, Swindon

Source: *North Wilts Herald* 18.08.1944, p.4
Evening Advertiser 12.07.1945, p.2

HOSKINS
RONALD SAMUEL GEORGE
ROYAL NAVY (HMS President III)
- Able Seaman
- Age: 23
- Died: 08.09.1944
- Buried in Radnor Street Cemetery, Swindon

Source: *Great Western Railway Magazine* November 1944, p.175
North Wilts Herald 16.07.1943, p.5 (photo)
North Wilts Herald 15.09.1944, p.8 (photo)
Evening Advertiser 11.09.44, p.4 (photo)

HOWARD
HAROLD HERBERT GEORGE
ROYAL AIR FORCE
- Sergeant Pilot
- Age: 24
- Died: 27.08.1940

Source: *Evening Advertiser* 29.04.1944, p.2
Lydiard Millicent War Memorial

HOWELL
EDWARD LEONARD
COLSTON
ROYAL AIR FORCE Voluntary Reserve
- Flight Sergeant
- Age: 31
- Died: 16.06.1944
- Attended Euclid Street School, Swindon

Source: *North Wilts Herald* 30.06.1944, p.4 (photo)
Evening Advertiser 26.06.1944, p.2 (photo)
Evening Advertiser 05.06.1945, p.2
Headlandian Summer 1946, p.30

HOWSE
ARTHUR ROBERT
ROYAL NAVY (HMS Barham)
- Chief Writer
- Died: 25.11.1941
- Wife came from Highworth

Source: *Evening Advertiser* 06.02.1942, p.4 (photo)

HUGHES
FREDERICK HENRY
WORCESTERSHIRE REGIMENT
- Private
- Age: 20
- Died: 8-9.05.1940
- Initially reported missing presumed killed
- Mother had written for information to Mrs Churchill

Source: *North Wilts Herald* 21.08.1942, p.3 (photo)
Evening Advertiser 15.08.1942, p.1 (photo)

HUMPHRIES
LESLIE JOHN
ROYAL NAVY (HMS Kipling)
- Able Seaman
- Age: 26
- Died: 11.05.1942

Source: *Great Western Railway Magazine* August 1946, p.183
Evening Advertiser 11.05.1944, p.2

HUNT
LAURIE
LEICESTERSHIRE REGIMENT
- Company Quartermaster Sergeant
- Age: 40
- Died: 03.01.1941
- Buried in South Marston (St. Mary Magdalene) Cemetery

Source: CWGC

HUNTER
RONALD WALLACE
ROYAL AIR FORCE Voluntary Reserve
- Leading Aircraftman
- Age: 21
- Died: 17.06.1940
- Lost on the R.M.S. Lancastria
- Attended Euclid Street School, Swindon

Source: *Evening Advertiser* 28.06.2010, p.23
Evening Advertiser 03.07.40, p.1 (photo)
Headlandian Summer 1946, p.30
ww2talk.com/forums/topic/14292-swindon-scouts-memorial/

HUTTON
GRANTLEY CHARLES
GEORGE
ROYAL AIR FORCE
Sergeant Flight Engineer
- Age: 19
- Died: 16.12.1942
- Initially reported missing, then killed in action

Source: *North Wilts Herald* 22.01.1943, p.5

Evening Advertiser 18.12.1942, p.1 (photo)

Evening Advertiser 18.01.1943, p.8 (photo)

I

ILES
ERNEST HENRY
ROYAL ENGINEERS
- Sapper
- Age: 36
- Died: 11.08.1946

Source: CWGC

ILES
ERNEST SIDNEY
WILTSHIRE REGIMENT
- Lance Corporal
- Age: 24
- Died: 10.07.1944

Source: *North Wilts Herald* 11.04.1944, p.7 (photo)
Evening Advertiser 16.07.1945, p.2

INKPEN
REGINALD SAM
ROYAL NAVY (HMS Hood)
- Stoker
- Age: 21
- Died: 24.05.1941

Source: *Evening Advertiser* 24.05.1945, p.2

ISAAC
JOHN A
ROYAL AIR FORCE
- Leading Aircraftsman
- Age: 33
- Died in Java POW camp

Source: *North Wilts Herald* 04.06.1943, p.4 (photo)
North Wilts Herald 03.12.1943, p.3 (photo)
Evening Advertiser 03.06.1943, p.8 (photo)
Evening Advertiser 30.11.1943, pp.2&5 (photo)
See Prisoners of War

IVERY
GEORGE FREDERICK
ROYAL NAVY (HMS Hydra)
- Petty Officer
- Age: 34
- Died: 10.11.1944

Source: *Evening Advertiser* 17.11.1944, p.2 (photo)

J

JACKSON
PETER FRANCIS
ROYAL AIR FORCE
Sergeant
- Age: 21
- Died: 07.05.1943

Source: *Great Western Railway Magazine* November 1943, p.172
North Wilts Herald 11.06.1943, p.4
North Wilts Herald 30.07.1943, p.8 (photo)
Evening Advertiser 29.07.1943 (photo)
Evening Advertiser 06.05.1944, p.2

JAMES
GILBERT
ROYAL ARTILLERY
- Signaller/Gunner
- Age: 24
- Died: 17.10.1942
- Accidentally electrocuted in Lebanon

Source: *Great Western Railway Magazine* January 1943, p.12
Wroughton War Memorial
www.roll-of-honour.com/wiltshire/wroughton
North Wilts Herald 06.11.1942, p.4 (photo)
Evening Advertiser 30.10.1942, p.8 (photo)
Wroughton History Group - Book 10 (2016), p.76

JAMES
I. C. G.
ROYAL NAVY
- Engineroom artificer

Source: *Great Western Railway Magazine* July 1942, p.132

JARMAN
JOHN SAMUEL
ROYAL AIR FORCE Voluntary Reserve
- Sergeant
- Died: 24.11.1944
- Buried in Christ Church Cemetery, Swindon

Source: *Evening Advertiser* 01.12.1944, p.6

JARVIE
THOMAS GUTHRIE
ROYAL TANK REGIMENT
- Trooper
- Age: 27
- Died: 07.09.1944

Source: CWGC

JARVIS
MELVILLE JOHN ERNEST
ROYAL AIR FORCE
- Leading Aircraftman
- Age: 22
- Died: 09.07.1940

Source: *North Wilts Herald* 03.01.1941, p.5
Evening Advertiser 30.12.1940, p.2

JEFFERIES
GRAHAM JOHN
ROYAL AIR FORCE
- Corporal
- Age: 24
- Died: 17.12.1944
- Died when a V2 rocket hit the Rex Cinema, Antwerp, Belgium

Source: Wroughton War Memorial
Evening Advertiser 29.12.1944, p.5 (photo)
Wroughton History Group - Book 10 (2016), p.75

JEFFERIES
PERCY HERBERT
AUSTRALIAN INFANTRY
- Private
- Age: 39
- Died: 30.10.1942
- Mother lived at 162 Ferndale Road, he emigrated to Australia about 1923

Source: *Evening Advertiser* 24.02.1943, p.3

JEFFERIES
ROBIN V
ROYAL ENGINEERS
- Sapper

Source: *Evening Advertiser* 17.05.1944, p.2

JENKINS
HENRY GEORGE
DUKE OF CORNWALL'S LIGHT INFANTRY
- Private
- Age: 28
- Died: 11.07.1944
- Attended Sanford Street School, Swindon

Source:*North Wilts Herald* 04.08.1944, p.8 (photo)
Evening Advertiser 29.7.1944, p.2 (photo)

JENNINGS
REGINALD E
ROYAL CORPS OF SIGNALS
- Signalman
- Age: 24
- Died: 18.07.1943
- Died of malaria while a POW in Thailand
- Attended Westcott Place School, Swindon

Source:*North Wilts Herald* 23.07.1943, p.5 (photo)
Evening Advertiser 16.07.1943, p.6 (photo)
Evening Advertiser 27.09.1943, p.8 (photo)
See Prisoners of War

JERVIS
JOHN HOWARD
ROYAL NAVY

Source:*Commonweal School Magazine* Summer 1944, p.5
Sanford Street Congregational Church memorial font, photo at Pilgrim Centre, Swindon

JOHNSON
ALAN MORETON
ROYAL AIR FORCE
- Warrant Officer/Air Gunner
- Age: 20
- Died: 12.06.1943
- Attended Clarence Street School, Swindon

Source:*North Wilts Herald* 12.06.1943, p.4 (photo)

JOHNSON
ERNEST GEORGE
ROYAL AIR FORCE Voluntary Reserve
- Aircraftsman 1st Class
- Died: 14.02.1945

Source: Bishopstone War Memorial

JONES
AUBREY ALLAN HAYES
ROYAL ENGINEERS
Sapper
- Age: 38
- Died: 22.11.1944
- *Evening Advertiser* says his wife is living with his mother in Wroughton, CWGC states Staffordshire
- Attended Wroughton School

Source: *Evening Advertiser* 05.12.1944, p.5 (photo)
Evening Advertiser 06.01.1945, p.3 (photo)
Wroughton History Group - Book 10 (2016), p.77

JONES
HENRY H
ROYAL AIR FORCE
- Warrant Officer
- Age: 36
- Died: 07.08.1942
- He and his wife were killed in the same incident
- Buried in Whitworth Road, Swindon

Source: CWGC

JONES
LESLIE CHARLES
ROYAL ARMY SERVICE CORPS
- Sergeant
- Age: 25
- Died: 04.07.1942

Source: *Headlandian* Summer 1946, p.30
Sanford St Congregational Church font, photo at Pilgrim Centre, Swindon

JONES
LEWIN JOHN
ROYAL NAVY (HMS Mohawk)
- Able Seaman
- Age: 37
- Died: 16.10.1939
- Killed by bomb splinters from a near miss during air raid on Firth of Forth

Source: *Evening Advertiser* 19.10.2009, p.17;
Evening Advertiser 23.10.1969, p.3 (photo)
Wroughton History Group - Book 10 (2016), p.77

JONES
MERLIN
ROYAL NAVY (HMS Chasseur 06)
- Stoker 1st class
- Age: 22
- Died: 12.10.1940

Source: *North Wilts Herald* 03.10.1941, p.5 (photo)
Evening Advertiser 22.10.1940, p.2 (photo)
Evening Advertiser 30.09.1941, p.3 (photo)

JONES
MERVYN ANTHONY
ROYAL AIR FORCE Voluntary Reserve Photographic Recon Unit
- Sergeant Pilot
- Age: 23
- Died: 03.04.1942
- Won Grand National 1940 on 'Bogskar',
- Nephew of Ivor Anthony, Marston House, Wroughton

Source:*Evening Advertiser* 11.04.1942, p.1
Wroughton History Group - Book 10 (2016), p.77

JONES
THOMAS JOHN
Military Police
- Private
- Age: 36
- Died: 13.10.1946
- Buried in Whitworth Road Cemetery, Swindon

Source: CWGC

JONES
THOMAS WILLIAM
ROYAL NAVY (HMS Daedalus)
- Naval Airman 2nd Class
- Age: 29
- Died: 18.04.1945
- Buried in Lower Stratton Cemetery, Swindon

Source: CWGC

JORDAN
ERNEST ALBERT LEONARD
ROYAL ARTILLERY/ COMMANDOS
- Officer Cadet/ Co Sgt Major
- Age: 25
- Died: 03.08.1945
- Attended Ferndale Road School, Swindon

Source: *Great Western Railway Magazine* October 1945, p.164
Evening Advertiser 25.04.1942, p.1
Evening Advertiser 09.08.1945, p.2

JORDAN
HAROLD WILLIAM FLEETWOOD
ROYAL AIR FORCE Voluntary Reserve
- Flight Engineer
- Age: 19
- Died: 04.12.1944
- Parents lived in Coleshill

Source: www.highworthhistoricalsociety.co.uk
Coleshill war memorial

JOSLING (DFC)
JOHN BASIL
ROYAL AIR FORCE Voluntary Reserve
- Flying Officer Pilot
- Age: 21
- Died: 24.07.44
- Husband of Patricia Josling of Lydiard Millicent
- Stirling bomber hit an oak tree and crashed killing all 9 on board

Source: CWGC
London Gazette 21.01.1944, p.429
See Awards and Medals

ROLL OF HONOUR 1939 – 1945

JOSLYN
GORDON WALLACE
ROYAL AIR FORCE
- Sergeant Air bomber
- Age: 20
- Died: 15.08.1944
- Attended Commonweal School, Swindon
- Brother of **KENNETH JOSLYN** (see below)

Source: *Commonweal School Magazine* Summer 1945, p.6
North Wilts Herald 06.10.1944, p.8 (photo)
Evening Advertiser 04.10.1944, p.5 (photo)

JOSLYN
KENNETH SIDNEY
ROYAL AIR FORCE Voluntary Reserve
- Sergeant Wireless Operator
- Age: 22
- Died: 14.01.1944
- Brother of **GORDON JOSLYN** (see above)

Swindon Town Football Club goalkeeper 1937-39
Source: *North Wilts Herald* 01.09.1944, p.2 (photo)
'Build me an Ark,' 1996, p.109
Evening Advertiser 04.10.1944, p.5

K

**KASPRZYNSKI
JANUSZ**
POLISH RESETTLEMENT
CORPS
- Private
- Age: 20
- Died: 02.09.1947
- Buried in Whitworth Road Cemetery, Swindon

Source: CWGC

**KEEN
WILLIAM**
ROYAL NAVY (HMS Rogate)
- Able Seaman
- Age: 43
- Died: 11.03.1941
- Buried in Radnor Street Cemetery, Swindon

Source: CWGC

**KEENAN
WILLIAM JOHN**
Source: St Barnabas Memorial Plaque, St Barnabas Church, Swindon

**KELSO
EDMUND STUART**
MERCHANT NAVY (SSWC Teagle)
- Chief Officer
- Age: 23
- Died: 16.10.1941

Source: CWGC

**KENDREW
CLARENCE**
ROYAL AIR FORCE Voluntary Reserve
- Sergeant Wireless Operator/Air Gunner
- Age: 20
- Died: 04.09.1943
- Buried in St Andrew's Churchyard Wanborough

Source: Wanborough War Memorial

**KENT
REGINALD HARRY**
ROYAL ARMY SERVICE CORPS
- Driver
- Age: 28
- Died: 13.06.1944
- Attended King William Street School, Swindon

Source: *North Wilts Herald* 14.07.1944, p.5 (photo)
Evening Advertiser 12.07.1944, p.1/2 (photo)
Evening Advertiser 13.06.1945, p.2

**KEOGH
MARTIN THOMAS MICHAEL**
ROYAL NAVY
- Ordnance Officer 3rd Class
- Age: 25
- Died: 27.05.1941
- Worked in Garrard's before the war
- Attended Swindon Secondary School

Source: *Swindonian* Summer 1941, p.878
North Wilts Herald 11.07.1941, p.5 (photo)
Evening Advertiser 05.07.1941, p.3 (photo)

KEYLOCK (MiD 2 Bars)
WILLIAM HENRY
ROYAL NAVY (HMS Penelope)
- Chief Petty Officer Telegraphist
- Age: 40
- Died: 18.02.1944
- Had completed his 30th bombing raid

Source:*North Wilts Herald* 29.03.1945, p.6 (photo)
North Wilts Herald 06.04.1944, p.4
North Wilts Herald 31.03.1944, p.5
See Awards and Medals

KIBBLEWHITE
ARTHUR SIDNEY
SUFFOLK REGIMENT
- Private
- Age: 34
- Died: 28.06.1944

Source: *North Wilts Herald* 28.04.1944, p.4
Evening Advertiser 28.06.1945, p.2

KILPATRICK
SAMUEL JAMES
ROYAL NAVY (HMS Dasher)
- Able Seaman
- Age: 19
- Died: 27.03.1943
- Father was formerly from Belfast, living at 36 Morris Street, Swindon in 1943

Source: *North Wilts Herald* 30.04.1943, p.8
Evening Advertiser 29.04.1943, pp. 2 & 4 (photo)
Evening Advertiser 29.03.1944, p.8

KIMBER
RONALD W
ROYAL NAVY (HMS Royal Arthur)
- Stoker 1st class
- Died: 27.05.1944
- Buried in Radnor Street Cemetery, Swindon

Source: St Augustine Church Memorial, Swindon

KIRBY
KATHLEEN MARY
AUXILLIARY TERRITORIAL SERVICE (ATS)
- Sergeant
- Age: 22
- Died: 08.09.1944

Source:*North Wilts Herald* 14.04.1944, p.8 (photo)
Evening Advertiser 11.09.1944, p.5 (photo)

KNIGHT
HAROLD
ROYAL AIR FORCE
- Leading Aircraftman
- Age: 21
- Died: 14.05.1944
- Attended Clarence Street School, Swindon

Source:*Great Western Railway Magazine* July 1944, p.110
Great Western Railway Magazine February 1945, p.32
North Wilts Herald 16.06.1944, p.4 (photo)
Evening Advertiser 12.06.1944, p.5 (photo)
Evening Advertiser 21.09.1944, p.4 (photo);
Evening Advertiser 14.05.1945, p.2

KNOWLER ARCHIE GERRARD
Pilot under training
- Age: 28
- Died: 27.01.1945
- Attended Euclid Street School, Swindon
- Was a Police Constable before enlisting

Source:*Headlandian* Summer 1945, p.22
Headlandian Summer 1946, p.30
Wiltshire Constabulary Memorial, London Road, Devizes

KOSLOWSKI WIESLAW
POLISH RESETTLEMENT CORPS
- Lance Corporal
- Age: 21
- Died: 03.11.1947
- Buried in Whitworth Road Cemetery, Swindon

Source:CWGC

KOSTITCH nee BABINGTON EILEEN
- Father had a drapers shop of Victoria Hill
- Joined guerrillas and fought with Tito against the Germans,
- Attended Commonweal School, Swindon

Source: *North Wilts Herald* 12.05.1944, p2 (photo)
Evening Advertiser 15.07.1941, p.2 (photo)
Evening Advertiser 11.05.1944, p.8 (photo)
Swindonian p.943

L

LAING (MiD & 2 bars)
DONALD
ROYAL AIR FORCE
- Flight Lieutenant
- Age: 34
- Died: 03.09.1942

Source: CWGC
See Awards and Medals

LANFEAR
RONALD
WILTSHIRE REGIMENT
- Corporal
- Age: 27
- Died: 11.06.1943

Source: Broad Hinton War Memorial

LAW
ALBERT
OXFORSHIRE AND BUCKINGHAMSHIRE LIGHT INFANTRY
- Corporal
- Age: 36
- Died: 16.06.1945
- A returned prisoner of war
- Father lived in Witts Lane, Purton

Source: War memorial in St Mary's Church, Purton
See Prisoners of War

LAWRANCE
LESLIE ARTHUR THOMAS
ROYAL ENGINEERS
Sapper
- Age: 24
- Died: 02.03.1943
- Killed in Middle East
- Attended King William Street School, Swindon

Source: *North Wilts Herald* 04.06.1943, p.8 (photo)
Evening Advertiser 02.06.1943, p.3 (photo)

LAWSON
JOHN LAWRENCE
ROYAL ARTILLERY
- Lieutenant
- Age: 32
- Died: 05.03.1943

Source: 'Millennium Memories' 2000 p.123

LAY
ERNEST
ROYAL NAVY
- Signalman
- Age: 19
- Died: 10.11.1944

Source: www.highworthhistoricalsociety.co.uk
Highworth Link November 2011, pp.4-5
Highworth War Memorial

LEA
NORMAN SIDNEY
ROYAL ARTILLERY/WELCH REGIMENT
- Private
- Age: 24
- Died: 31.12.1944
- Attended Jennings Street School, Swindon

Source:*Great Western Railway Magazine* March 1945, p.48
St. Augustine Church Memorial, Swindon
North Wilts Herald 12.01.1945, p.8
Evening Advertiser 10.19.1945, p.2/5 (photo)

LEANEY
LEN
ROYAL AIR FORCE
- Sergeant Air Gunner
- Died: 05.05.1943
- *Evening Advertiser* lists him as missing from May 1943

Source:*Evening Advertiser* 07.03.1944, p.2

LEAVER
PHILLIP HARRIS
ROYAL AIR FORCE
- Flying Officer (Pilot)
- Age: 24
- Died: 16.02.1946
- Buried in Whitworth Road Cemetery, Swindon

Source:CWGC

LEGG
ARTHUR GEORGE (JIM)
KINGS SHROPSHIRE LIGHT INFANTRY
- Private
- Age: 21
- Died: 01.03.1945
- Attended Pinehurst School, Swindon

Source:*North Wilts Herald* 23.03.1945, p.8 (photo)

LEVY
JOHN
ROYAL ARMY SERVICE CORPS
- Driver
- Age: 24
- Died: 11.04.1945

Source:CWGC

LEWIN
FREDERICK ROBERTS ALEXANDER
IRISH GUARDS
- Lieutenant
- Age: 25
- Died: 15.05.1940
- Grandson of Lord Roberts, family lived at Salthrop House, Wroughton
- Left £47,000 in his will
- His troopship was attacked in Norwegian waters

Source:*North Wilts Herald* 24.05.1940, p.7
Evening Advertiser 20.05.1940, p.1
Evening Advertiser 27.11.1940, p.3
North Wilts Herald 09.05.1941, p.8

LEWINGTON
JAMES
ROYAL ARTILLERY
- Gunner
- Age: 32
- Died: 26.02.1943
- He was a member of Gorse Hill Working Men's Club, Swindon

Source: *North Wilts Herald* 20.08.1943, p.6 (photo)
Evening Advertiser 16.08.1943, p.8 (photo)
Evening Advertiser 21.08.1943, p.8
Evening Advertiser 26.02.1944, p.2

LEWIS
ALBERT CORNELIUS
ROYAL ENGINEERS
- Sapper
- Age: 18
- Died: 28.07.1945
- Died in Clitheroe
- Buried in Whitworth Road Cemetery, Swindon

Source: *Evening Advertiser* 01.08.1945, p.2

LEWIS
SIDNEY GEORGE
QUEEN'S ROYAL REGIMENT
- Sergeant
- Age: 34
- Died: 22.10.1944
- Attended Gorse Hill School, Swindon

Source:*North Wilts Herald* 24.11.1944, p.8 (photo)
Evening Advertiser 20.11.1944, p.8 (photo)

LLOYD
ALLAN A
ROYAL AIR FORCE
- Sergeant (Wireless Operator/Air Gunner)
- Age: 20
- Died: 23.02.1941
- Attended Commonweal School
- Buried in Christ Church Cemetery, Swindon

Source: *North Wilts Herald* 28.02.1941, p.5 (photo)
Evening Advertiser 24.02.2011
Evening Advertiser 26.02.1941 p.3;
Evening Advertiser 23.02.1944, p.2
Evening Advertiser 23.02.1951, p.6
Commonweal School Magazine Summer 1941, p.6

LLOYD
GRAHAM
- Died in accident in Devonport Dockyard where he'd been drafted in lieu of serving in force
- Believed to be from Purton
- Attended Euclid Street School, Swindon

Source: *Headlandian* Summer 1946, p.30

LOGUE
JAMES
ROYAL AIR FORCE Voluntary Reserve
- Leading Aircraftman
- Age: 36
- Died: 06.02.1946
- Buried in Whitworth Road Cemetery, Swindon, plot G356

Source:CWGC

ROLL OF HONOUR 1939 – 1945

LOOKER
LESLIE JOHN
ROYAL NAVY (HMS Barham)
- Chief Stoker
- Age: 34
- Died: 25.11.1941

Source: CWGC

LOSS
HORACE
BEDFORDSHIRE AND
HERTFORDSHIRE REGIMENT
- Private
- Age: 32
- Died: 27.07.1943

Source: CWGC

LOVE
MAURICE HENRY
ROYAL ARTILLERY
- Gunner /Driver Mechanic
- Age: 20
- Died: 22.07.1944
- Attended Gorse Hill School, Swindon

Source: *North Wilts Herald* 25.08.1944, p.5 (photo)
Evening Advertiser 19.08.1944, p.1 (photo)
Evening Advertiser 21.07.1945, p.2
Evening Advertiser 24.07.1945, p.2

LOVE
RONALD ALEXANDER
ROYAL BERKSHIRE
REGIMENT
- Private
- Age: 31
- Died: 22.03.1943

Source: *Evening Advertiser* 22.03.1944, p.2

LOVEDAY
ALEXANDER TREVOR
MIDDLESEX REGIMENT
- Private
- Age: 19
- Died: 19.04.1945
- Buried in Christ Church Cemetery, Swindon

Source: CWGC

LUKINS
EDWARD CHARLES
WILTSHIRE REGIMENT
- Private
- Age: 21
- Died: 04.09.1940
- Son of Mr and Mrs W J Lukins, of Wroughton

Source: CWGC

M

MCCARTHY (DFM)
ROBERT WILLIAM
ROYAL AIR FORCE
- Leading Aircraftman
- Age: 24
- Died: 06.12.1942
- Attended Euclid Street School, Swindon

Source: *The Euclidean* Summer 1943
The Euclidean Christmas 1943
North Wilts Herald 28.06.1940, p.3
Evening Advertiser 21.06.2010, p.16
Evening Advertiser 25.06.1940, p.3
Headlandian Summer 1946, p.30
See Awards and Medals

MACLOUGHLIN
FRANK GORDON
ROYAL NAVY (HMS Vervain)
- Leading Stores Assistant
- Age: 20
- Died: 02.1945
- Killed while on convoy duty
- Worked at Garrard's

Source: *North Wilts Herald* 06.07.1945, p.8 (photo)
Evening Advertiser 01.07.1945, p.2

MADDEN
JOHN
GORDON HIGHLANDERS
- Warrant Officer class 1/ CSM
- Age: 36
- Died: 19.01.1943
- Died of wounds received at El Alamein

Source: *Evening Advertiser* 19.01.1944, p.2

MAISEY
JACK ERNEST WILLIAM
ROYAL MARINES
- Marine
- Age: 21
- Died: 22.09.1944
- Attended Clarence Street School, Swindon

Source: *Great Western Railway Magazine* December 1944, p.192
Stratton Green Baptist Church Memorial
North Wilts Herald 13.10.1944, p.8 (photo)
Evening Advertiser 07.10.1944, p.5 (photo)

MAJOR
FREDERICK JOHN
WILTSHIRE REGIMENT
- Sergeant
- Age: 24
- Died: 21.04.1944
- Died of wounds
- Attended Sanford Street School, Swindon

Source: *Great Western Railway Magazine* July 1944, p.110
15 Shop Memorial, STEAM, Swindon
North Wilts Herald 05.05.1944, p.5 (photo)
Evening Advertiser 03.05.1944, p.5 (photo)

MAPSON
GEORGE WILLIAM
ROYAL NAVY
- Petty Officer
- Age: 26
- Died: 01.02.1943
- Parents lived at 170 Marlborough Road
- Killed while serving on HMS Welshman

Source:*Evening Advertiser* 08.02.1943, p.4 (photo)
Evening Advertiser 2.02.1944, p.2

MARCHANT
RICHARD JOHN (JACK)
ROYAL AIR FORCE Voluntary Reserve
- Aircraftsman 2nd class
- Age: 20
- Died: 19.02.1941
- Killed in flying accident
- Ex butcher with Keylocks in Wood Street
- Brother from Clanfield killed on submarine Narwhal

Source: *Evening Advertiser* 24.02.2011
North Wilts Herald 28.02.1941, p.2 (photo)

MARSDEN
JOHN
ROYAL AIR FORCE Voluntary Reserve
- Sergeant Air Gunner
- Age: 34
- Died: 23.03.1944
- Killed in a flying accident in Northamptonshire
- Attended Rodbourne Cheney School, Swindon

Source: *North Wilts Herald* 31.03.1944, p.8
Evening Advertiser 26.01.1945, p.2
Evening Advertiser 25.03.1944, p.8
Evening Advertiser 27.03.1944, p.2

MARTIN
THOMAS
QUEEN'S OWN CAMERON HIGHLANDERS
- Corporal
- Age: 30
- Died: 07.05.1944
- Died at Kohima, India during the Burma campaign

Source: CWGC

MASLEN
ARTHUR LEONARD
ROYAL AIR FORCE Voluntary Reserve
- Sergeant
- Age: 21
- Died: 26.01.1942
- Killed in air operations over Singapore
- Attended Swindon Secondary School

Source: *Swindonian* Autumn 1941, p.886
Great Western Railway Magazine April 1942, p.85
North Wilts Herald 20.02.1942, p.5 (photo)
Evening Advertiser 18.02.1942, p.3 (photo)
Evening Advertiser 26.01.1944, p.2

MASON
WILLIAM ROBERTSON
PIONEER CORPS
- Private
- Age: 35
- Died: 24.12.1943
- Buried in Lower Stratton Cemetery

Source: CWGC

MATTHEWS
CECIL EDWARD
WILTSHIRE REGIMENT
- Private
- Age: 32
- Died: 12.06.1942
- Buried in St Mary's Churchyard, Purton

Source: *Great Western Railway Magazine* January 1943, p.12

MATTHEWS (DFM)
DOUGLAS SPENCER
ROYAL AIR FORCE
- Pilot Officer
- Age: 23
- Died: 09.01.1942
- Attended Swindon Secondary School
- Buried in Christ Church, Swindon
- Manchester aircraft R5789 was on raid over docks at Cherbourg when 1 engine died and other misfired. Captain and 2nd pilot kept aircraft steady while all crew bailed out. Both killed attempting to crash land.
- Brother to **GORDON MATTHEWS**, see Prisoners of War

Source: *Swindonian* Autumn 1941, p.886
Evening Advertiser 14.1.1942, p.3
Evening Advertiser 15.1.1942, p.4
North Wilts Herald 16.01.1942, p.3 (photo)
Evening Advertiser 18.05.1945, p.2
See Awards and Medals

MATTHEWS
STANLEY WILLIAM
ROYAL AIR FORCE (Voluntary Reserve)
- Aircraftman 1st class
- Age: 26
- Died: 13.02.1942
- Missing at sea
- Parents lived at Quarry Farm, Purton

Source: War memorial in St Mary's Church, Purton

MATTICK (DFM)
STANLEY RICHARD
ROYAL AIR FORCE Voluntary Reserve
- Flight Sergeant
- Died: 02.01.1944

Source:*North Wilts Herald* 22.10.1943, p.6 (photo)
North Wilts Herald 29.03.1945, p.6 (photo)
North Wilts Herald 16.03.1945, p.5 (photo);
Evening Advertiser 18.10.1943, p.8 (photo)
Evening Advertiser 07.01.1944, p.1
Evening Advertiser 15.01.1944, p.3
Stratton Green Baptist Church Memorial
See Awards and Medals

MAYBURY
DONALD CONRAD
ROYAL AIR FORCE
- Flying Officer
- Age: 23
- Died: 12.04.1940
- Attended Swindon Secondary School

Source:*Swindonian* Summer 1940, p.859
Evening Advertiser 12.04.2010
North Wilts Herald 19.04.1940
North Wilts Herald 26.04.1940, p.12
Evening Advertiser 17.04.1940, p.1 (photo)
Evening Advertiser 18.04.1940, p.1 (photo)

MEADER
GORDON ARTHUR
ROYAL NAVY (HMS Escapade)
- Able Seaman
- Age: 19
- Died: 20.09.1943
- Attended Gorse Hill School, Swindon

Source:*North Wilts Herald* 01.10.1943, p.6 (photo)
Evening Advertiser 24.09.1943, p.8 (photo)

MEES
WILFRED HENRY
ROYAL ELECTRICAL AND MECHANICAL ENGINEERS
- Driver
- Age: 24
- Died: 11.08.1944

Source: CWGC

MIDDLETON
JOHN DEREK (DEREK)
ROYAL AIR FORCE
- Flight Lieutenant
- Died: 09.07.1940
- Served with 201 Squadron, the flying boat squadron
- Failed to return from a mission

Source: *Evening Advertiser* 11.07.1940, p.1

MIDDLETON
WALLACE
ROYAL NAVAL RESERVE (HMS Rawalpindi)
- Midshipman
- Age: 17
- Died: 23.11.1939
- Attended Euclid Street School, Swindon

Source: *Evening Advertiser* 23.11.2009, p.16
Evening Advertiser 27.11.1939, p.1 (photo)
Evening Advertiser 28.11.1939, p.1
Evening Advertiser 29.11.1939, p.1
Evening Advertiser 12.01.1940, p.1

MILES
HENRY CHARLES
CAMBRIDGESHIRE REGIMENT
- Private
- Age: 30
- Died: 31.07.1943
- Died while a prisoner of war in Singapore

Source: www.highworthhistoricalsociety.co.uk
Highworth War Memorial
See Prisoners of War

MILLS
RAYMOND EWART (CURLY)
ROYAL NAVY (HMS Hood)
Stoker 2nd class
- Age: 23
- Died: 24.05.1941

Source: *Evening Advertiser* 24.05.1944, p.2

MITCHELL
EWART CECIL
ROYAL AIR FORCE
- Leading Aircraftman
- Age: 20
- Died: 04.10.1944
- *Evening Advertiser* lists him as 'missing presumed killed'.
- Attended Euclid Street School, Swindon

Source: *Great Western Railway Magazine* July 1945, p.117
North Wilts Herald 13.07.1945, p.4
Evening Advertiser 11.07.1945, p.2
Headlandian Summer 1946, p.30

MITCHELL
H.J.
ROYAL CORPS OF SIGNALS
- Signalman
- Age: 21
- Died: 26.06.1947

Source: CWGC

MOODY
HAROLD VICTOR
WILTSHIRE REGIMENT
- Private
- Age: 22
- Died: 10.08.1944

Source: *Great Western Railway Magazine* November 1944, p.175

MOORE
LAURENCE THOMAS
ROYAL AIR FORCE Voluntary Reserve
- Leading Aircraftman
- Age: 25
- Died: 03.10.1942

Source: CWGC

MORGAN
CYRIL JAMES
ROYAL AIR FORCE Voluntary Reserve
- Warrant Officer
- Age: 30
- Died: 12.09.1942
- Cyril's parents (Isaac and Martha) lived at 21 Plymouth Street, Swindon
- Cyril's wife Martha lived in Birmingham then moved to Cornwall

Source: CWGC

MORGAN
JOHN
LOVAT SCOUTS
- Warrant Officer (RSM)
- Age: 43
- Died: 26.12.1946
- Buried in Radnor Street Cemetery, Swindon

Source: CWGC

MORGAN
KENNETH DUCK
ROYAL NAVY (HMS Rawalpindi)
- Lieutenant Commander
- Age: 35
- Died: 23.11.1939
- Nephew of Mr T Read of Brown and Plummers

Source: *Evening Advertiser* 27.11.1939, p.1

MORGAN
WALTER JOHN
ROYAL AIR FORCE Voluntary Reserve
- Sergeant/Navigator
- Age: 29
- Died: 15.07.1944
- Buried in Whitworth Road Cemetery, Swindon
- Attended Even Swindon School, Swindon

Source: St Augustine Church Memorial
North Wilts Herald 21.07.1944, p.5 (photo)
Evening Advertiser 18.07.1944, p.4 (photo)
Evening Advertiser 14.07.1945, p.2

MORRIS
MARTIN STANLEY
ROYAL AIR FORCE Voluntary Reserve
- Flying Officer (Pilot)
- Age: 24
- Died: 07.01.1943
- Great grandson of William Morris

Source: *North Wilts Herald* 05.02.1942, p.3 (photo)
Evening Advertiser 04.02.1943, pp.2/4 (photo)

MORRISON
DESMOND CYRIL
ROYAL AIR FORCE Voluntary Reserve
- Sergeant Wireless Operator/Air Gunner
- Age: 19
- Died: 21.03.1941
- Attended Lethbridge Road School, Swindon
- Died in flying accident
- Buried in Christ Church Cemetery, Swindon

Source: *Evening Advertiser* 24.03.1941, p.4
Evening Advertiser 29.03.1941, p.3

MORSE
STANLEY CARLTON
ROYAL AIR FORCE Voluntary Reserve
- Sergeant Gunner
- Died: 05.07.1941
- Son of W. E. Morse of The Croft, Swindon
- Missing after bombing raid in Germany

Source: *North Wilts Herald* 15.08.1941, p.2 (photo)
Evening Advertiser 09.07.1941, p.2 (photo)
Evening Advertiser 14.08.1941, p.4 (photo)

MORTON
CYRIL JOHN
ROYAL NAVY (HMS Exmouth)
- Warrant Officer
- Died: 21.01.1940
- Attended Swindon Secondary School

Source: *Swindonian* Summer 1940, p.859

MOSS
TOM A.
ROYAL ENGINEERS
Sapper
- Age: 22
- Died: 01.12.1942
- Died in a prisoner of war camp in Germany as result of an accident

Source: *Great Western Railway Magazine* December 1941, p.328
Great Western Railway Magazine January 1945, p.15
Evening Advertiser 05.02.1942, p.2 (photo)
North Wilts Herald 05.10.1941, p.8
See Prisoners of War

MOULDEN (MiD)
NORMAL CHARLES
FLEET AIR ARM (HMS Newcastle)
- Leading Aircraftman
- Age: 21
- Died: 01.11.1941
- Attended Westcott Place School, Swindon

Source: *North Wilts Herald* 14.11.1941, p.5 (photo)
Evening Advertiser 06.11.1941, p.4
Evening Advertiser 07.11.1941, p.3
See Awards and Medals

MOYNIHAN
PATRICK
QUEEN'S VICTORIA RIFLES
- Rifleman
- Age: 26
- Died: 07.10.1943
- Buried in Radnor Street Cemetery, Swindon

Source: CWGC

MULLIS
GRAHAM GLYNNE
ROYAL ARTILLERY
- Gunner
- Age: 26
- Died: 03.10.1944
- Attended Sanford Street School, Swindon

Source: Wroughton War Memorial
North Wilts Herald 03.11.1944, p.5 (photo)
Evening Advertiser 14.10.1944, p.8
Evening Advertiser 28.10.1944, p.1 (photo)
Wroughton History Group - Book 10 (2016), p.77

N

NEAL
EDWARD RICHARD (EDDIE)
ROYAL NAVY (HMS Hood)
- Supply Assistant
- Died: 24.05.1941
- Lost on HMS Hood

Source: 'In Memoriam', 1946, Swindon Press (photo)
Evening Advertiser 24.05.1944, p.2
Evening Advertiser 24.05.1945, p.2

NEATE
ROBERT SPENCER
ROYAL AIR FORCE
- Flight Sergeant Pilot
- Died: 09.07.1945
- Attended Commonweal School, Swindon

Source: *Commonweal School Magazine* Summer 1946, p.4

NEVILLE
NORMAN REGINALD
ROYAL NAVY (HMS Dorsetshire)
- Ordinary Telegraphist
- Age: 19
- Died: 05.04.1942
- Attended Gorse Hill School, Swindon

Source: *Evening Advertiser* 01.05.1942, p.3 (photo)

NEW
FREDERICK FRANCIS JAMES
DUKE OF CORNWALL'S LIGHT INFANTRY
- Corporal
- Age: 27
- Died: 10.05.1941
- Buried in Whitworth Road Cemetery, Swindon

Source: *Evening Advertiser* 10.05.1944, p.2

NEWMAN
GORDON SIDNEY
MIDDLESEX REGIMENT
- 2nd Lieutenant
- Died: between 8 and 25.12.1942
- Killed in action in Hong Kong
- Attended Commonweal School, Swindon

Source: *Swindonian* Summer 1942, p.3
St Augustine Church Memorial
North Wilts Herald 28.08.1942, p.5 (photo)
Evening Advertiser 25.08.1942, p.4 (photo)

NEWMAN
RICHARD HARRY
ROYAL ENGINEERS
- Sapper
- Died: 21.03.1940
- Buried in Christ Church Cemetery, Swindon

Source: CWGC

NICHOLS
ALBERT EDWARD
WILTSHIRE REGIMENT
- Private
- Age: 29
- Died: 05.08.1943
- Killed in Sicily
- Attended Blunsdon Village School

Source: Blunsdon War Memorial
North Wilts Herald 03.09.1943, p.6 (photo)
Evening Advertiser 30.08.1943, p.2 (photo)

NORRIS
FRANK WILLIAM BATES
ROYAL AIR FORCE Voluntary Reserve
- Flight Sergeant/Air Gunner
- Age: 20
- Died: 05.06.1944
- Failed to return from an exercise over the North Sea on the day before D-Day

Source: *Great Western Railway Magazine* August 1946, p.183
North Wilts Herald 16.06.1944, p.3 (photo)
Evening Advertiser 15.06.1944, p.2 (photo)
Evening Advertiser 23.01.1945, p.2
Evening Advertiser 05.10.1945, p.2
Swindon Heritage Autumn 2016, p.52

O

**OCKWELL
ALEXANDER ERNEST**
ROYAL ARTILLERY
- Gunner
- Died: 05.04.1940
- Buried in Whitworth Road Cemetery, Swindon

Source: *Great Western Railway Magazine* June 1940. p.199

**OCKWELL
CHRISTOPHER THOMAS**
ROYAL MARINES
- Marine
- Age: 23
- Died: 18.01.1944

Source: *Great Western Railway Magazine* April 1944, p.66
19C Shop Memorial, STEAM, Swindon

**OCKWELL
HERBERT VICTORY (VIC)**
ARMY AIR CORPS (Wing Glider Pilot Regiment)
- Staff Sergeant
- Age: 27
- Died: 06.06.1944
- Killed in action at Merville Battery on D Day
- Family information says he was killed during Operation Tonga when his glider crashed into an anti-landing pole.
- Glider was carrying 5 sappers from 591 Parachute Squadron, Royal Engineers, jeep, trailer, motorcycle, bridging sections and a war correspondent

Source: Highworth War Memorial
www.highworthhistoricalsociety.co.uk

**O'CONNELL
ARTHUR DANIEL**
ROYAL NAVY
- Wireman
- Age: 19
- Died: 25.04.1943
- Killed when 2 invasion barges sank off coast of Wales
- Attended Commonweal School, Swindon

Source: *North Wilts Herald* 07.05.1943, p.4 (photo)
Evening Advertiser 03.05.1943, p.5 (photo)
Evening Advertiser 05.11.1943, p.8

ODEY
EDWARD CHARLES
WILTSHIRE REGIMENT
- Private
- Age: 18
- Died: 24.03.1946

Source: CWGC

OLIVER
ALBERT ALEXANDER
AIR TRANSPORT AUXILLERY
- Radio Operator
- Died: 10.08.1941
- Killed in plane crash over Scotland, with 22 other servicemen

Source: *Evening Advertiser* 13.08.1941, p.1 (photo)

OLNEY
JAMES FREDERICK
COLDSTREAM GUARDS
- Lance Sergeant
- Age: 30
- Died: 14.09.1944
- Played for Swindon Town Football Club

Source: *Evening Advertiser* 12.07.1945, p.8
Evening Advertiser 14.07.1945, p.2

O'NEIL
LIONEL HENRY
MERCHANT NAVY (SS Avoceta)
- 4th Engineer Officer
- Age: 29
- Died: 25.09.1941

Source: CWGC

OSTLER
WILLIAM CLIFFORD
ROYAL ARMY ORDNANCE CORPS
- Private
- Age: 39
- Died: 14.09.1941

Source: *Great Western Railway Magazine* December 1941, p.328

OTTIGNAN
CHARLES VIVIAN
ROYAL NAVY (HMS Sub Salmon)
- Able Seaman
- Age: 20
- Died: 09.07.1940

Source: CWGC

P

PACKER
HAROLD JOHN (DARKIE)
WILTSHIRE REGIMENT
- Private
- Age: 31
- Died: 15.04.1944
- Killed in action in Burma

Source:*North Wilts Herald* 06.10.1944, p.8 (photo)
Evening Advertiser 26.04.1944, p.2 (photo)
See Awards and Medals

PAGE
JOSEPH HENRY
DUKE OF CORNWALL'S LIGHT INFANTRY
- Private
- Age: 27
- Died: 01.06.1940
- Drowned during evacuation from France, one of 5 brothers serving

Source: *Evening Advertiser* 05.07.2010, p.16
North Wilts Herald 12.07.1940
Evening Advertiser 09.07.1940, p.3 (photo)
Evening Advertiser 24.02.1940, p.3

PAINTIN
GEORGE WILLIAM
THE BLACK WATCH
- Lance Corporal
- Age: 25
- Died: 24.10.1944
- Attended Jennings Street School, Swindon

Source:*North Wilts Herald* 01.12.1944, p.5 (photo)

PALMER
BERNARD OCTAVIUS DREW
ROYAL MARINES
- Lieutenant
- Age: 37
- Died: 02.04.1942

Source:CWGC

PALMER
HORACE OSBORNE
ROYAL NAVY (HMS Birmingham)
- Able Seaman (cook)
- Age: 35
- Died: 28.11.1943
- Attended Gorse Hill School, Swindon

Source:*North Wilts Herald* 10.12.1943, p.5 (photo)
Evening Advertiser 25.11.1944, p.5 (photo)
Evening Advertiser 06.12.1943, p.4 (photo)
Evening Advertiser 29.12.1943, p.2

PARKER
ROBERT
ROYAL ENGINEERS
- Sergeant
- Age: 30
- Died: 23.08.1944
- CWGC states he was in Gordon Highlanders

Source: *Evening Advertiser* 02.10.1944, p.2
Evening Advertiser 03.10.1944, p.4
Evening Advertiser 24.12.1944, p.2 (photo)
North Wilts Herald 23.03.1945, p.8 (photo)

PARRETT
DONALD WILLIAM
ROYAL AIR FORCE Voluntary Reserve
- Leading Aircraftman
- Age: 26
- Died: 14.12.1941
- Parents lived at 26 Wood St. CWGC says they were from Brixham
- Attended Swindon High School
- Parents presented High School with a cup in son's memory.

Source:*North Wilts Herald* 19.12.1941, p.5 (photo)
North Wilts Herald 30.01.1942, p.5
Evening Advertiser 30.01.1942, p.3 (photo)
Swindon Scout Memorial
Christ Church War Memorial

PARSONS
HENRY WILILAM JAMES
ROYAL NAVY (HMS Thracian)
- Petty Officer Stoker
- Died: 19.12.1941

Source:St Augustine Church Memorial

PAYNE
ROBERT JAMES
DUKE OF WELLINGTON'S REGIMENT
- Private
- Age: 21
- Died: 23.02.1942
- Attended Clarence Street School Swindon

Source:*North Wilts Herald* 10.04.1942, p.6
Evening Advertiser 02.04.1942, p.1 (photo)

PEBWORTH (DFC)
DENIS ARTHUR
ROYAL AIR FORCE Voluntary Reserve
- Flight Lieutenant (Observer)
- Age: 22
- Died: 24.08.1942
- Attended Sanford Street School, Swindon
- Buried in Whitworth Road Cemetery, Swindon

North Wilts Herald 28.08.1942, p.8 (photo)
North Wilts Herald 04.09.1942, p.3
North Wilts Herald 30.10.1942, p.5 (photo)
Evening Advertiser 29.08.1942, p.3 (photo)
Evening Advertiser 28.10.1942, p.4 (photo)
Evening Advertiser 04.03.1943, p.1 (photo) shows parents collecting DFC from Buckingham Palace
Wills Works Magazine, Aug 1945, p.14
Wills Factory plaque in St Luke's Church, Swindon
See Awards and Medals

PERRIN
WILLIAM RONALD (RON)
ROYAL ARTILLERY
- Gunner
- Age: 22
- Died: 09.04.1943
- Attended Rodbourne Cheney School, Swindon

Source: *Evening Advertiser* 01.05.1943, p.1
Evening Advertiser 06.05.1943, P.2 (photo)
Evening Advertiser 08.04.1944, p.2

PERRY
LEONARD FREDERICK (PETER)
ROYAL ARTILLERY
- Gunner
- Died: 16.02.1944
- Died of wounds resulting from a lorry accident
- Buried in Whitworth Road Cemetery, Swindon

Source:*Evening Advertiser* 21.02.1944, p.1 (photo)
Evening Advertiser 22.02.1944, p.6

PERRY
ROBERT JOHN
ROYAL ARTILLERY Warrant Officer
- Age: 30
- Died: 13.08.1944
- Buried in Whitworth Road Cemetery

Source: *Evening Advertiser* 13.08.1945, p.2

PETERS
CHARLES WILLIAM
PIONEER CORPS
- Private
- Age: 30
- Died: 07.02.1944
- Parents lived in Lambourne

Source: Swindon High School Memorial in Christ Church, Swindon

PHILLIPS
NORMAN ROBERT
ROYAL ENGINEERS
- Sapper
- Died: 21.02.1946
- Killed in motorbike accident
- Buried in Whitworth Road Cemetery, Swindon

Source:*Great Western Railway Magazine* May 1946, p.110
19B Shop Memorial, STEAM, Swindon
See Prisoners of War

PICKERING
ALBERT EDWARD
LINCOLNSHIRE REGIMENT
- Corporal
- Age: 41
- Died: 31.08.1944
- Buried in St Andrew's Church, Wanborough

Source: CWGC

PICTON
RAYMOND KENNETH
GLIDER PILOT REGIMENT AAC
- Staff Sergeant
- Age: 23
- Died: 25.09.1944

Source: CWGC

PIKE
HERBERT WILLIAM GEORGE
ROYAL MARINES
- Marine
- Age: 42
- Died: 01.03.1941
- Lost at sea
- Lived with sister in Rodbourne from 1937

Source: *North Wilts Herald* 27.06.1941, p.2 (photo)

PONTIN
FRANK
- Private
- Brother of **REGINALD PONTIN** see below, son of Sidney Pontin of Chiseldon

Source: *Evening Advertiser* 14.05.1945, p.2

PONTIN
REGINALD SIDNEY
QUEEN'S ROYAL REGIMENT
- Lance Serjeant
- Age: 24
- Died: 17.12.1944
- Brother of **FRANK PONTIN** see above, son of Sidney Pontin of Liddington and Chiseldon
- Attended Chiseldon School

Source: *Evening Advertiser* 02.01.1945, p.5 (photo)
Evening Advertiser 14.05.1945, p.2

PONTING
CLIFFORD HERBERT
ROYAL ARMOURED CORPS
(9th Queen's Royal Lancers)
- Trooper
- Age: 22
- Died: 30.05.1942
- Commemorated on El-Alamein memorial

Source: CWGC

PONTING
GEORGE
ROYAL SUSSEX REGIMENT
- Private
- Age: 23
- Died: 06.08.1944

Source: CWGC

POOLE
ALLAN JOHN
ROYAL NORFOLK REGIMENT
- Private
- Age: 26
- Died: 14.08.1944
- Buried in Hong Kong

Source: CWGC

POOLE
WILLIAM ROBERT
QUEEN'S OWN CAMERON HIGHLANDERS
- Private
- Age: 28
- Died: 20.08.1944
- Parents lived in Hinton Parva, Wiltshire

Source: CWGC

POPE
GERALD MONTEITH
ROYAL ENGINEERS (601 Railway Construction Company)
- Sapper
- Age: 22
- Died: 21.04.1942

Source: CWGC

POPE
IVOR ALECK
ROYAL ARTILLERY
- Gunner
- Age: 35
- Died: 29.11.1943
- Died as result of the sinking of a Japanese transport vessel (Suez Maru) on which he, together with other POWs, was being transferred from Java to another prisoner of war camp
- Attended Even Swindon School, Swindon

Source: St Augustine Church Memorial
North Wilts Herald 28.05.1943, p.7 (photo)
North Wilts Herald 28.01.1944, p.4 (photo)
Evening Advertiser 21.05.1943, p.2 (photo)
Evening Advertiser 27.01.1944, p.1 (photo)
See Prisoners of War

PORTER
HAROLD
ROYAL ARTILLERY
- Sergeant
- Age: 34
- Died: 18.09.1944

Source: *North Wilts Herald* 25.02.1944, p.4 (photo)
Evening Advertiser 28.09.1944, p.5 (photo)
Wills Works Magazine, August 1945, p.16
Wills Works Magazine, March 1946, p.17
Will's factory plaque in St Luke's Church, Swindon

POTTER
ERNEST STANLEY
KINGS SHROPSHIRE LIGHT INFANTRY
- Private
- Age: 21
- Died: 03.06.1944

Source: St Augustine Church Memorial
North Wilts Herald 14.07.1944, p.8 (photo)
Evening Advertiser 12.07.1944, p.3 (photo)
Evening Advertiser 02.06.1945, p.2

POTTER
JOHN
ROYAL ARMOURED CORPS
- Corporal
- Age: 31
- Died: 29.05.1940

Source: CWGC

POWELL
CLIFFORD WILLIAM
MORGAN
ROYAL AIR FORCE Voluntary Reserve
- Flight Lieutenant
- Age: 23
- Died: 01.11.1942
- Attended Clarence Street School, Swindon

Source: *Great Western Railway Magazine* January 1943, p.12
Evening Advertiser 06.11.1942, p.4 (photo)

PRICE
JACK ERIC
ROYAL AIR FORCE
- Aircraftman 2nd class
- Age: 18
- Died: 21.09.1943
- Buried in Whitworth Road Cemetery, Swindon

Source: *Great Western Railway Magazine* November 1943, p.172
19B Shop Memorial, STEAM, Swindon

PRIESTMAN
HAROLD ROBINSON
ROYAL AIR FORCE Voluntary Reserve
Sergeant Pilot
- Died: 05.08.1943
- Buried in All Saints Church, Faringdon

Source: 'In Memoriam', 1946, Swindon Press 1946 (photo)

PULLEN
JAMES
Corporal
Age: 37
Source: *North Wilts Herald* 18.08.1944, p.4

Q

QUARRELL (DSM) WILLIAM (HAROLD)
ROYAL NAVY (HM Submarine Tigris)
- Petty Officer
- Age: 29
- Died: 10.03.1943

Source: *North Wilts Herald* 03.03.1944, p.8 (photo)
Evening Advertiser 18.11.1943, p.2
Evening Advertiser 02.03.1944, p.4 (photo)
See Awards and Medals

QUINCE WALTER ERNEST (WALLY)
ROYAL AIR FORCE Voluntary Reserve
- Sergeant Pilot
- Age: 20
- Died: 01.11.1941
- Died when his Hurricane crashed while returning from patrol over Bristol Channel, 4 days after his 20th birthday
- Attended Euclid Street School, Swindon
- Buried in Whitworth Road Cemetery, Swindon

Source: *Great Western Railway Magazine* February 1942, p.45
Evening Advertiser 06.11.1941, p.4
North Wilts Herald 07.11.1941, p.2 (photo)
Headlandian Summer 1946, p.30

R

RAVEN
SIDNEY GEORGE
COLDSTREAM GUARDS
- Sergeant
- Age: 33
- Died: 12.10.1944
- Son of Charles Edward Raven of Malvern Road, Swindon
- Attended St Barnabas Church

Source: CWGC

RAWLINGS
DENNIS REGINALD GEORGE
ROYAL ARTILLERY
- Gunner
- Age: 21
- Died: 18.07.1944
- Died of wounds received in Italy

Source: *Evening Advertiser* 03.08.1944, p.5 (photo)
Evening Advertiser 18.07.1945, p.2

REES
HENRY FRANCIS
WILTSHIRE REGIMENT
- Private
- Age: 31
- Died: 10.07.1944

Source: CWGC

RENDALL
VICTOR
MERCHANT NAVY (SS Empire Beresford)
- 5th Engineer Officer
- Age: 24
- Died: 03.10.1947
- Buried in Whitworth Road Cemetery, Swindon

Source: CWGC

REYNOLDS (DFM)
BERNARD ALLAN
ROYAL AIR FORCE
- Sergeant Pilot
- Age: 24
- Died: 08.08.1944
- Attended Commonweal School

Source: *Swindonian* Summer 1945, p.6
North Wilts Herald 18.08.1944, p.5 (photo)
Evening Advertiser 11.08.1944, p.8 (photo)
Evening Advertiser 19.06.1943, p.1 (photo)
Evening Advertiser 01.12.1943, p.8 (photo)
North Wilts Herald lists him as missing
See Awards and Medals

REYNOLDS
DONALD
WILTSHIRE REGIMENT
- Private
- Age: 19
- Died: 23.01.1945

Source: *Wroughton History Group Book 7*, (1997) p.8

RICE
GEORGE LEONARD
ROYAL NAVY (HMMTB 444)
- Stoker 1st class
- Age: 20
- Died: 14.02.1945

Source: CWGC

RICH
TREVOR
ROYAL AIR FORCE
- Flying Officer (Navigator)
- Age: 23
- Died: 21.07.1944

Attended Commonweal School, Swindon
Source: St Augustine Church Memorial
Evening Advertiser 20.07.1945, p.2

RICHENS
GEORGE WILLIAM
SOMERSET LIGHT INFANTRY
- Private
- Age: 24
- Died: 30.06.1944

Source: *North Wilts Herald* 21.07.1944, p.5
Evening Advertiser 15.07.1944, p.2
Evening Advertiser 30.06.1945, p.2

RICHINGS
THOMAS MONTAGUE
ROYAL AIR FORCE Voluntary Reserve (RNZAF Squadron)
- Wireless Operator/Air Gunner
- Age: 22
- Died: 06.12.1942
- Wife came from Swindon

Source: CWGC

RICHMAN
PETER
ROYAL AIR FORCE
- Sergeant Wireless Officer
- Age: 30
- Died: 09.03.1945
- Killed in flying accident near Stafford
- Attended Lethbridge Road School, Swindon

Source: *North Wilts Herald* 16.03.1945, p.5 (photo)

RICKARD-BELL
H.M
ROYAL AIR FORCE Voluntary Reserve
- Sergeant

Source: *Evening Advertiser* 18.11.1942, p.5

RIDLEY
JAMES ASHDOWN
DUKE OF CORNWALL'S LIGHT INFANTRY
- Private
- Age: 26
- Died: 16.04.1943
- Died of wounds in South Africa

Source: *Evening Advertiser* 25.05.1943, p.5

RISHTON
NORMAN
ROYAL HORSE ARTILLERY
- Lance Sergeant
- Age: 29
- Died: 31.10.1942
- Buried in El-Alamein

Source: CWGC

**RIVERS
ERIC**
ROYAL ARTILLERY
- Driver
- Age: 26
- Died: 21.02.1945
- Killed in a 'battle accident'

Source: *North Wilts Herald* 09.03.1945, p.4

**RIVERS
WILFRED**
ROYAL TANK REGIMENT
- Trooper
- Died: 24.11.1942

Source: CWGC

**ROBBINS
EDGAR R.**
ROYAL ENGINEERS
- Lance Corporal
- Age: 21
- Died: 20.05.1941

Source: *Great Western Railway Magazine* July 1941, p.187
North Wilts Herald 06.06.1941, p.5 (photo)
Swindonian Summer 1941, p.878
Evening Advertiser 20.05.1944, p.2
Evening Advertiser 19.05.1945, p.2

**ROBBINS
GEOFFREY NEIL**
MONMOUTHSHIRE REGIMENT
- Private
- Age: 22
- Died: 20.07.1944
- Attended Holy Rood School, Swindon

Source: *Evening Advertiser* 14.08.1944, p.2 (photo)

**ROBINSON
DOUGLAS GRAHAM**
THE BLACK WATCH
- Private
- Age: 21
- Died: 08.08.1944

Source: Wroughton War Memorial
Evening Advertiser 30.08.1944, p.2 (photo)
Wroughton History Group - Book 10 (2016), p.78

**ROBINSON
FREDERICK GEORGE**
ROYAL NAVY (HMS Phoenix)
- Leading Air Mechanic
- Age: 27
- Died: 08.08.1943
- Died following an accident which fractured his skull
- Attended Wroughton School

Source: *North Wilts Herald* 27.08.1943, p.3 (photo)
Evening Advertiser 24.08.1943, p.4 (photo)

**ROBINSON
JOHN**
ROYAL ARMOURED CORPS
- Sergeant
- Age: 32
- Died: 10.03.1945
- Buried in Whitworth Road Cemetery, Swindon

Source: CWGC

ROBINSON
WALTER GEORGE ALBERT
Grenadier Guards
- Guardsman
- Age: 21
- Died: 31.02.1944
- Killed on the Italian front
- Attended Clifton Street School, Swindon

Source: *Evening Advertiser* 19.02.1944, p.5 (photo)

ROCHESTER
AUBREY (EDGAR) PERRIN
ROYAL AIR FORCE Voluntary Reserve
- Sergeant
- Age: 33
- Died: 24.05.1943
- Failed to return after operation over Dortmund
- Attended Euclid Street School, Swindon

Source: *The Euclidean* Christmas 1943
Evening Advertiser 24.05.1944, p.2
Evening Advertiser 24.05.1942, p.2
Source: *Headlandian* Summer 1946, p.30
Wroughton History Group - Book 10 (2016), p.78

ROE
FRANK FREEMAN (JIM)
PIONEER CORPS (formerly of ROYAL ARTILLERY)
- Major
- Age: 56
- Died: 08.09.1945

Source: CWGC

ROGERS
CLAUDE VERNON
ROYAL NAVY (HMS Cape Howe)
- Stoker 1st class
- Age: 24
- Died: 21.06.1940

Source: CWGC

ROLFE
LESLIE PERCY CHARLES
ROYAL AIR FORCE Voluntary Reserve
Sergeant Wireless Operator/Air Gunner
- Age: 21
- Died: 15.06.1941
- Attended Clifton Street School, Swindon

Source: *North Wilts Herald* 30.01.1942, p.3
Evening Advertiser 25.07.1941, p.1 (photo)
Evening Advertiser 29.01.1942, p.4 (photo)

ROSE
ALBERT EDWARD
WILTSHIRE REGIMENT
- Private (Despatch Rider)
- Age: 27
- Died: 04.07.1944
- Attended Sanford Street School, Swindon

Source: *North Wilts Herald* 04.08.1944, p.5 (photo)
Evening Advertiser 28.07.44, p.2 (photo)
'Build me an Ark', *Crossfire*, 1996, p.109

ROSS
FREDERICK BARTON
ROYAL ENGINEERS
- Sapper
- Age: 44
- Died: 20.03.1945

Source: CWGC

ROUND (DFM)
FRANK DESMOND
ROYAL AIR FORCE
- Flight Lieutenant
- Age: 26
- Died: 05.07.1944
- Husband of Frances Round of Highworth

Source: CWGC
London Gazette 22.08.1941, p.4865
See Awards and Medals

ROUT
SIDNEY CHARLES
ARMY CATERING CORPS
- Private
- Died: 19.10.1943
- Died of burns in North Africa following the explosion of a primus stove.
- His parents lived in Highworth

Source: www.highworthhistoricalsociety.co.uk
Highworth War Memorial

RUSSELL
FRANCIS EDWARD
ROYAL NAVY (HMS Coventry)
- Stoker 1st class
- Died: 14.09.1942

Source: *Great Western Railway Magazine* November 1942, p.196
15 Shop Memorial, STEAM, Swindon

RUSSELL
FRANK GEORGE
ROYAL ARTILLERY
- Gunner
- Age: 34
- Died: 15.08.1944

Source: CWGC

RYAN (GC)
RICHARD JOHN HAMMERSLEY
ROYAL NAVY (HMS President)
- Lieutenant Commander
- Age: 37
- Died: 21.09.1940
- Husband of Margaret Ryan, of Wroughton
- George Cross Citation on CWGC

Source: CWGC
see Awards and Medals

S

SADLER
JOHN
ROYAL NAVY
- Engineer
- Lived at 16 Wiltshire Avenue, Swindon
- Attended Gorse Hill School, Swindon

Source: *North Wilts Herald* 02.10.1942, p.5 (photo)
Evening Advertiser 01.10.1942, p.5 (photo)

SANSUM
IVOR JOHN
ROYAL AIR FORCE
Warrant Officer
- Age: 26
- Died: 07.10.1946
- Reported missing 23.07.1943
- Buried in Christ Church Cemetery, Swindon

Source: *Great Western Railway Magazine* December 1946, p.279
North Wilts Herald 23.07.1943, p.5 (photo)

SAUNDERS
JOHN JAMES
ROYAL ENGINEERS
- Sapper
- Age: 30
- Died: 03.12.1940
- Buried in Whitworth Road Cemetery, Swindon

Source: CWGC

SCOTT
ROBERT CHARLES
ROYAL MARINES (HMS Hood)
- Marine
- Age: 26
- Died: 24.05.1941
- Died in the sinking of HMS Hood

Source: CWGC

SCOTT
WILLIAM GORDON
ROYAL ARMY SERVICE CORPS
- Driver
- Age: 29
- Died: 07.11.1942
- Lived at 21 Rodbourne Road and parents lived at Thomas Street
- Attended Even Swindon School, Swindon

Source: *North Wilts Herald* 27.11.1942, p.5 (photo)
Evening Advertiser 23.11.1942, p.1 (photo)

SCOTT-BROWNE
KENNETH WILLIAM
KINGS OWN SCOTTISH BORDERERS 7th Airborne Battalion
- Private
- Age: 23
- Died: 04.04.1944
- Accidentally killed
- Buried in Radnor Street Cemetery, Swindon

Source: *Evening Advertiser* 06.04.1944, p.8

SEALY/SEALEY
JOHN CHARLES WILLIAM
ROYAL AIR FORCE Voluntary Reserve
Sergeant Pilot
- Age: 21
- Died: 24.06.1942
- Attended Euclid Street School, Swindon
- Buried in Radnor Street Cemetery, Swindon

Source: *Great Western Railway Magazine* August 1942, p.149
Evening Advertiser 23.06.1945, p.2
Headlandian Summer 1946, p.30

SELWOOD
HERBERT WALTER JAMES
ROYAL ARTILLERY
- Gunner
- Age: 37
- Died: 10.02.1945

Source: *North Wilts Herald* 23.07.1943, p.8 (photo)
North Wilts Herald 02.03.1945. p.4 (photo)
Evening Advertiser 20.07.43, p.4 (photo)
North Wilts Herald 23.03.1945, p.8 (photo)
See Prisoners of War

SHAW
FRANCIS ELLIOTT
- ROYAL AIR FORCE Voluntary Reserve Sergeant/Pilot
- Age: 24
- Died: 22.04.1941
- Buried in Whitworth Road Cemetery, Swindon

Source: CWGC

SHEWRY
MABEL FLORENCE ETHEL
WOMEN'S AUXILIARY AIR FORCE
- Aircraftwoman 1st Class
- Age: 26
- Died: 25.03.1946
- Buried in Upper Stratton Cemetery

Source: CWGC

SIDDERS
FREDERICK ERNEST
GRENADIER GUARDS
- Corporal
- Age: 23
- Died: 28.10.1943
- Parents lived in Purton

Source: CWGC

SIMMONS
VICTOR GEORGE
ROYAL FUSILIERS
- Corporal
- Age: 24
- Died: 12.05.1944
- Died at Monte Cassino

Source: www.highworthhistoricalsociety.co.uk
Highworth War Memorial

SIMMONDS
ROY HECTOR PANNELL
SOMERSET LIGHT INFANTRY
- Private
- Age: 30
- Died: 12.05.1944
- Died at Monte Cassino

Source: CWGC

**SIMPKINS
ALBERT LEONARD**
OXFORDSHIRE AND
BUCKINGHAMSHIRE LIGHT
INFANTRY
- Private
- Age: 24
- Died: 19.01.1944
- Attended Westcott Place School, Swindon

Source:*Evening Advertiser* 23.02.1944, p.5 (photo)

**SIMPKINS
LIONEL VICTOR**
ROYAL ARMOURED CORPS
- Trooper
- Age: 22
- Died: 22.10.1942
- Attended Even Swindon School, Swindon

Source:*Great Western Railway Magazine* January 1943, p.12
St Augustine Church Memorial
North Wilts Herald 06.11.1942, p.3 (photo)
Evening Advertiser 05.11.1942, p.1 (photo)

**SIMS
HENRY WARNEFORD**
ROYAL ARTILLERY
- Gunner
- Age: 28
- Died: 08.02.1944
- Attended Upper Stratton School

Source: *North Wilts Herald* 01.09.1944, p.2 (photo)
Evening Advertiser 29.02.1944, p.5 (photo)

**SLADE
RALPH WILLIAM**
ROYAL AIR FORCE Voluntary Reserve
- Leading Aircraftman
- Age: 20
- Died: 26.12.1941
- Buried in Whitworth Road Cemetery, Swindon

Source:*North Wilts Herald* 09.01.1942, p.7
Evening Advertiser 03.01.1942, p.2
Evening Advertiser 24.12.1943, p.2

**SLATER
ERNEST FREDERICK**
DUKE OF CORNWALL'S
LIGHT INFANTRY
- Company Quartermaster Sergeant
- Age: 42
- Died: 11.06.1945

Source: CWGC

**SLATER
ERNEST LESLIE**
ROYAL AIR FORCE Voluntary Reserve
- Leading Aircraftman
- Died: 15.05.1945
- Buried in Whitworth Road Cemetery, Swindon

Source:CWGC

**SMITH
ALBERT CHARLES**
GLOUCESTER REGIMENT
- Private
- Age: 34
- Died: between 19-24.05.1940

Source: CWGC

SMITH
ALBERT GEORGE
ROYAL NAVY (HM Sub Porpoise)
- Stoker 1st class
- Age: 21
- Died: 16.01.1945

Source: www.highworthhistoricalsociety.co.uk

SMITH
D.J.
ROYAL ARMY ORDNANCE CROPS
- Corporal

Source: *Great Western Railway Magazine* June 1946, p.131

SMITH
DENNIS HAROLD
ROYAL EAST KENT REGIMENT (The Buffs)
- Private
- Age: 24
- Died: 13.04.1945

Source: www.highworthhistoricalsociety.co.uk
Highworth War Memorial

SMITH
EDGAR WALLACE
ROYAL NAVY (HMS Victory)
- Stoker 1st class
- Age: 46
- Died: 10.03.1941

Source: Post Office Memorial, Swindon
www.royalmailmemorials.com/memorial/swindon-postal-district-war-memorial

SMITH
GEORGE ARTHUR
MERCHANT NAVY (SS Baltrader)
- Able Seaman
- Age: 28
- Died: 09.11.1940
- Gunner on SS Baltrader which struck a mine off the Kent coast

Source: www.highworthhistoricalsociety.co.uk

SMITH
HERBERT JOHN
WILTSHIRE REGIMENT
- Lieutenant
- Died: 01.06.1944
- Killed at Anzio

Source: Highworth Link November 2011 pp.4-5
Evening Advertiser 16.06.1944, p.5
www.highworthhistoricalsociety.co.uk

SMITH
HUBERT KENNETH
ROYAL AIR FORCE
- Flying Officer, Pilot Instructor
- Age: 26
- Died: 07.04.1942
- Worked for Wiltshire Newspapers
- Attended Commonweal School, Swindon
- Buried in Christ Church Cemetery, Swindon

Source: *Swindonian* Summer 1944, p.5
'In Memoriam', 1946, Swindon Press (photo)
North Wilts Herald 10.04.1942, p.5 (photo)
Evening Advertiser 08.04.1942, p.4 (photo)
Evening Advertiser 10.04.1942, p.4

SMITH
JOHN HOWARD
ROYAL AIR FORCE Voluntary Reserve
Sergeant/Wireless Operator
- Age: 20
- Died: 15.12.1944

Source: CWGC

SMITH (MM and Bar)
JOSEPH GEORGE
WILTSHIRE REGIMENT
- Regimental Sergeant Major
- Age: 32
- Died: 16.02.1945

Source: *North Wilts Herald* 27.10.1944, p.5
North Wilts Herald 27.10.1944, p.5
North Wilts Herald 02.03.1945, p.4 (photo)
Evening Advertiser 09.09.1944, p.8 (photo)
Evening Advertiser 21.10.1944, p.5
Evening Advertiser 25.05.1945, p.1
Stanton Fitzwarren War Memorial
See Awards and Medals

SMITH
MICHAEL STACEY CLARE
ROYAL AIR FORCE
- Flying Officer
- Age: 21
- Died: 04.10.1944
- Attended Swindon High School
- Believed to have been shot down by night-fighter off the Dutch coast during a reconnaissance sortie

Source: *Evening Advertiser* 14.10.1944, p.5 (photo)
Swindon High School Memorial in Christ Church, Swindon
Swindon Scout Memorial
ww2talk.com/forums

SMITH
SIDNEY ANDREW
ROYAL NAVY
- Petty Officer
- Age: 21

Source: *North Wilts Herald* 04.04.1941, p.2 (photo)
Memorial in St Augustine Church, Swindon
Evening Advertiser 25.03.1944, p.2
Evening Advertiser 02.04.1941, p.1 (photo)

SMITH
STANLEY GEORGE
QUEEN'S OWN ROYAL WEST KENT REGIMENT
- Private
- Age: 23
- Died: 27.07.1944
- Killed in Italy

Source: www.highworthhistoricalsociety.co.uk
Highworth War Memorial

SMITTEN
HARRY
ROYAL NORFOLK REGIMENT
- Private
- Age: 26
- Died: 01.09.1943
- Buried in Burma

Source: *Evening Advertiser* 02.04.1942, p.4 (photo)
Evening Advertiser 02.06.1943, p.5 (photo)
North Wilts Herald 20.08.1943, p.6
See Prisoners of War

SNEWING
GEORGE JAMES HARRY
ROYAL AIR FORCE Voluntary Reserve
- Flight Sergeant
- Age: 22
- Died: 18.08.1945

Source: CWGC

SPARROW
WILLIAM JAMES
ROYAL NAVY (HM Sub P33)
- Chief Engineroom Artificer
- Age: 37
- Died: 20.08.1941

Source: CWGC

SPENCER
JOSEPH HENRY
ROYAL ARTILLERY
- Gunner
- Age: 25
- Died: 10.11.1943
- Buried in Whitworth Road Cemetery, Swindon

Source: CWGC

SPRUCE
STANLEY
ROYAL NAVY (HMS Prince of Wales)
- Boy 1st class
- Age: 17
- Died: 10.12.1941
- HMS Prince of Wales was sunk by Japanese bombers, north of Singapore on 10.12.1941

Source: CWGC

SQUIRES
ALFRED ERNEST WILLIAM
ROYAL PIONEER CORPS
- Private
- Age: 45
- Died: 17.06.1947
- Buried in Whitworth Road Cemetery, Swindon

Source: CWGC

STAFFORD
ALFRED JOSEPH
ROYAL ARTILLERY
- Gunner
- Age: 28
- Died: 24.05.1947

Source: CWGC

STARR
HAROLD MORLEY
ROYAL AIR FORCE
- Squadron Leader
- Age: 26
- Died: 31.08.1940
- Brother of **NORMAN STARR**, see below
- Shot while baling out of aircraft
- Parents ran the Central Hotel, Regent Street
- Funeral described in *Evening Advertiser* 07.09.1940
- Attended Clarence Street School, Swindon
- Buried in Radnor Street Cemetery, Swindon

Source: *Evening Advertiser* 02.09.1940 p.1
Evening Advertiser 03.09.1940, p.4
Evening Advertiser 07.09.1940 p.1
Swindon Heritage magazine, special edition September 2015

STARR (DFC and Bar)
NORMAN JOHN
ROYAL AIR FORCE
- Wing-Commander (pilot)
- Age: 28
- Died: 08.01.1945
- Brother of **HAROLD STARR**, see above
- Reported missing 8.01.1945, known killed and buried at Dunkirk 09.06.1945

Source: *North Wilts Herald* 16.04.1943, p.5
North Wilts Herald 15.06.1945, p.5
Evening Advertiser 09.04.1943, p.5
Evening Advertiser 09.06.1945, p.2
Swindon Heritage magazine, special edition September 2015
Memorial in Radnor Street Cemetery, Swindon
See Awards and Medals

STEPHENS
CYRIL WILTSHIRE
ROYAL BERKSHIRE REGIMENT
- Lieutenant
- Died: 09.05.1944

Source: *North Wilts Herald* 09.06.1944, p.8 (photo)
Evening Advertiser 05.06.1944, p.2 (photo)

STEVENS
CYRIL MAURICE
ROYAL ARTILLERY
- Gunner
- Age: 32
- Died: 23.07.1943
- Buried in St Mary's Churchyard, Rodbourne Cheney

Source: CWGC

STOCK
ARTHUR ERNEST
ROYAL NAVY (HMS Afrikander IV)
- Able Seaman
- Age: 23
- Died: 18.10.1942

Source: CWGC

STONE
RAYMOND STANLEY
PARACHUTE REGIMENT, ARMY AIR CORPS
- Private
- Age: 23
- Died: 15.04.1945
- Buried in Chiseldon Cemetery, Wiltshire

Source: CWGC

STRANGE
GEORGE ROBERT (BOB)
WILTSHIRE REGIMENT
- Lance Corporal
- Age: 36
- Died: 04.05.1944

Source: *North Wilts Herald* 02.06.1944, p.5 (photo)
Evening Advertiser 29.05.1944, p.2 (photo)

STRINGER
GEORGE ROBERT
ROYAL ENGINEERS
- Sapper
- Age: 28
- Died: 12.11.1943

Source: CWGC

STROUD
DOUGLAS EDWARD HENRY
ROYAL AIR FORCE
- Leading Aircraftman
- Age: 23
- Died: 24.07.1943

Source: *Great Western Railway Magazine* August 1946, p.183
15 Shop Memorial, STEAM, Swindon

STUNELL
HERBERT
ROYAL ARTILLERY
- Quartermaster Sergeant
- Age: 28
- Died: 21.10.1941
- Buried in Watchfield Cemetery

Source: CWGC

SWEET
WILLIAM JOHN
DEVONSHIRE REGIMENT
- Private
- Age: 35
- Died: 31.07.1943

Source: CWGC

T

TAME
ALBERT LIONEL
ROYAL AIR FORCE
- Aircraftman 2nd class
- Age: 21
- Died: 16.11.1943
- Died in prisoner of war camp in Java
- Attended Highworth School

Source: www.highworthhistoricalsociety.co.uk
Evening Advertiser 01.01.1944, p.4 (photo)
North Wilts Herald 07.01.1944, p.6
Highworth War Memorial
See Prisoners of War

TAYLOR
ERNEST JOHN
CAMBRIDGESHIRE REGIMENT
- Private
- Age: 32
- Died: 15.05.1943
- Parents lived in Purton

Source: CWGC

TAYLOR
FRANK ALBERT
ROYAL ENGINEERS
- Lance Sergeant
- Age: 29
- Died: 02.11.1944

Source:*Evening Advertiser* 13.11.1944, p.2

TAYLOR
JOHN
ROYAL ARMY MEDICAL CORPS
- Sergeant
- Age: 37
- Died: 01.11.1946
- Buried in Whitworth Road Cemetery, Swindon

Source:CWGC

TAYLOR
PERCIVAL JOHN
ROYAL TANK REGIMENT
- Corporal
- Age: 28
- Died: 02.05.1941
- Buried near Tobruk

Source:*Evening Advertiser* 02.05.1944, p.2

THATCHER
ALFRED CHARLES
ROYAL NAVY (HMS Dorsetshire)
- Petty Officer (Cook)
- Age: 36
- Died: 05.04.1942

Source:CWGC

THATCHER
ROBERT THOMAS
ROYAL NAVY (HMS Gloucester)
- Engineroom Artificer 4th class
- Age: 25
- Died: 22.05.1941

Source: CWGC

THEOBALD
LEONARD CHARLES
WILTSHIRE REGIMENT
- Private
- Age: 28
- Died: 23.02.1942
- Killed in a 'friendly fire' incident
- Buried in Whitworth Road Cemetery, Swindon

Source: *Evening Advertiser* 23.02.1951, p.6

THOMAS
JAMES VICTOR LEWIS
ROYAL AIR FORCE
- Leading Aircraftman
- Age: 28
- Died: 17.06.1940
- Died on the R.M.S. Lancastria

Source: Swindon Heritage Magazine Winter 2016, pp.24-28

THOMPSON
ALBERT EDWARD
ROYAL NAVY (HMS Stag)
- Stoker
- Age: 34
- Died: 08.03.1941

Source: *North Wilts Herald* 21.03.1941, p.5
Evening Advertiser 18.03.1941, p.3 (photo)
Evening Advertiser 08.03.1943 p.2
Evening Advertiser 11.03.1944, p.2

THOMPSON
ARTHUR JOSEPH
CAMBRIDGESHIRE REGIMENT
- Private
- Age: 22
- Died: 16.02.1942

Source: *Great Western Railway Magazine* May 1946, p.110
Evening Advertiser 08.04.1942, p.3 (photo)

THORNHILL
WILFRED
ROYAL AIR FORCE Voluntary Reserve
- Flight Sergeant
- Age: 23
- Died: 25.04.1941

Source: CWGC

TIMMS
HAROLD PERCIVAL
ROYAL NAVY (HMS Nubian)
- Able Seaman
- Age: 21
- Died: 06.04.1943

Source: *Evening Advertiser* 06.04.1945, p.2
Evening Advertiser 06.04.1944, p.2
Wills Works Magazine August 1945, p.16
Wills Works Magazine March 1946, p.19
Listed on Wills factory plaque in St Luke's Church, Swindon

TITCHENER
STANLEY VICTOR
ROYAL AIR FORCE
- Sergeant
- Age: 22
- Died: 16.05.1946
- Killed in flying accident after end of war
- Buried in Whitworth Road Cemetery, Swindon

Source: *Great Western Railway Magazine* August 1946, p.183
Headlandian Summer 1946, p.30

TITCOMB (DSM)
ERNEST ARTHUR ROBERT
ROYAL NAVY (HMS Searcher)
- Petty Officer
- Age: 34
- Died: 22.01.1945
- Father (Alfred William Titcomb) from Rodbourne, died in WW1

Source: Wroughton War Memorial
www.roll-of-honour.com/wiltshire/wroughton
Evening Advertiser 27.11.1942, p.1 (photo)
Wroughton History Group - Book 10 (2016), pp.79 & 102
See Awards and Medals

TOOMBS
WILLIAM ERNEST
ROYAL NAVY (HMS St Fagan)
- Able Seaman
- Died: 01.06.1940
- Lost on tug St Fagan during evacuation of Dunkirk
- Attended Clifton Street School, Swindon

Source: *Evening Advertiser* 04.06.1940, p.1
Evening Advertiser 01.06.1945, p.2

TOWNSEND
CLIFFORD HARRY
ROYAL NAVY (HMS Belmont)
- Stoker 1st class
- Age: 24
- Died: 31.01.1942
- Not brother of Francis or Sidney Townsend also listed
- Lived in Cricklade Road, Swindon

Source: CWGC

TOWNSEND
FRANCIS RICHARD (FRANK)
ROYAL NAVY (HMS Rajputana)
- Able Seaman
- Age: 22
- Died: 13.04.1941
- HMS Rajputana torpedoed off Iceland
- Not brother of Sidney or Clifford Townsend, Presumed dead 07.07.41

Source: *North Wilts Herald* 11.07.1941, p.3
Evening Advertiser 07.07.1941, p.2 (photo)
Evening Advertiser 13.04.1945, p.2
Evening Advertiser 13.04.1944, p.2

TOWNSEND
SIDNEY JAMES
ROYAL ARTILLERY
- Gunner
- Age: 37
- Died: 26.07.1943
- Not brother of Francis or Clifford Townsend

Source: *Great Western Railway Magazine* November 1943, p172

TRINEMAN
KENNETH JOHN
ROYAL NAVAL VOLUNTEER
RESERVE (HMS Malnerian)
- Acting Sub Lieutenant
- Age: 25
- Died: 02.07.1941

Source: *Evening Advertiser* 06.07.41, p.4

TROLLOPE
RONALD WILLIAM
ROYAL ARTILLERY
- Bombardier
- Age: 28
- Died: 11.04.1943
- Buried in Whitworth Road Cemetery, Swindon

Source: CWGC

TRUEMAN
MONTAGUE JAMES (JIM)
PARACHUTE REGIMENT
- Private
- Age: 21
- Died: 06.06.1944
- Killed on D Day

Source: *Evening Advertiser* 06.06.1945, p.2

TUCK
PERCY JAMES
QUEEN'S ROYAL REGIMENT (WEST SURREY)
- Lance Corporal
- Age: 24
- Died: 10.09.1943
- Parents lived in Purton

Source: CWGC

TUNSTALL
RICHARD
ROYAL ENGINEERS
- 2nd Lieutenant
- Attended Westcott Place School, Swindon

Source: *Evening Advertiser* 04.07.1940, p.4
Evening Advertiser 11.07.1940, p.4

TURNBULL
STANLEY
ROYAL ARTILLERY
- Gunner
- Attended Clifton Street School, Swindon

Source: *Great Western Railway Magazine* February 1944, p.32
North Wilts Herald 31.12.1944, p.8 (photo)
Evening Advertiser 28.12.1943, p.5 (photo)

TYRELL
CHARLES FREDERICK
ROYAL ARTILLERY
- Bombardier
- Age: 25
- Died: 14.08.1944

Source: CWGC

UV

**URQUHART
ALLAN FRANK**
ROYAL ARTILLERY
- Gunner
- Age: 38
- Died: 31.07.1942
- Buried in Lower Stratton Cemetery

Source: CWGC

**VAN DER WEYER
ADRIAN JOHN BATES**
RIFLE BRIGADE
- 2nd Lieutenant
- Age: 20
- Died: 26.05.1940
- Nephew of Major and Mrs Bates of The Manor, South Marston

Source: *North Wilts Herald* 01.11.1940, p.8

W

WAKEFIELD
ALBERT JOHN
SUFFOLK REGIMENT
- Private

Source: Lydiard Millicent War Memorial

WALDRON
JAMES ROY
ROYAL AIR FORCE Voluntary Reserve
- Pilot Officer
- Age: 22
- Died: 12.09.1943
- Attended Euclid Street School, Swindon
- Buried in Whitworth Road Cemetery, Swindon
- Was a Police Constable before enlisting

Source: *The Euclidean* Christmas 1943
North Wilts Herald 17.09.1943, p.5 (photo)
Headlandian Summer 1946, p.30
Wiltshire Constabulary Memorial, London Road, Devizes

WALKER
ALFRED VICTOR
ROYAL ARMY SERVICE CORPS
- Lance Corporal
- Age: 35
- Died: 17.09.1943
- Killed while evacuating wounded from Salerno

Source: *Evening Advertiser* 08.10.1943, p.2
Evening Advertiser 05.06.1945, p.2

WALKER (DSM)
LESLIE NORMAN
ROYAL NAVY (HMS Isis)
- Able Seaman
- Age: 25
- Died: 20.07.1944
- Attended Clarence Street School, Swindon

Source: *Great Western Railway Magazine* November 1944, p.175
Great Western Railway Magazine November 1945, p.182
North Wilts Herald 03.08.1945, p.8 (photo)
Evening Advertiser 09.08.1944, p.2 (photo)
Evening Advertiser 31.07.1945, p.2
See Awards and Medals

WALTON
WILLIAM LESLIE
WILTSHIRE REGIMENT
- Lieutenant
- Age: 29
- Died: 18.03.1945

Source: St Augustine Church Memorial, Swindon

WARR
ALFRED THOMAS STANLEY
ROYAL ENGINEERS
- Sapper
- Age: 21
- Died: 20.05.1940

Source: *Great Western Railway Magazine* July 1940, p.223

WARREN
STANLEY
ROYAL ELECTRICAL AND
MECHANICAL ENGINEERS
- Craftsman
- Age: 29

Source: *Evening Advertiser*
18.08.1944, p.4 (photo)
Evening Advertiser 30.07.1945, p.2

WATTS
SIDNEY ROY
ROYAL ARMY MEDICAL
CORPS
- Private
- Age: 19
- Died: 14.10.1947
- Buried in Radnor Street Cemetery, Swindon

Source: CWGC

WATTS
WILLIAM HAROLD
ROYAL NAVY (HMS Kite)
- Supply Assistant
- Age: 37
- Died: 21.08.1944
- Attended Clarence Street School, Swindon

Source: *Evening Advertiser*
22.09.1944, p.5 (photo)

WEBB
EDWARD
ROYAL ARTILLERY
- Lance bombardier
- Age: 22
- Died: 12.07.1943
- Killed in Sicily

Source: *North Wilts Herald*
06.08.1943, p.5 (photo)
Evening Advertiser 03.08.1943, p.4 (photo)
Evening Advertiser 12.07.1945, p.8
Wills Works Magazine August 1945, p.16
Wills Works Magazine March 1946, p.19
Wills factory plaque in St Luke's Church, Swindon

WEBB
ERIC JOSEPH LESLIE
ROYAL NAVY (HMS TRINDAD)
- Cook
- Age: 22
- Died: 15.05.1942

Source: Bishopstone War Memorial
Further information supplied by family

WEBB
SIDNEY BERNARD
ROYAL ARMY SERVICE CORPS
- Driver
- Age: 22
- Died: 01.10.1944
- Attended Ferndale Road School, Swindon
- CWGC lists him as a Private in the Dorset Regiment

Source: *Great Western Railway Magazine* December 1944, p.193
North Wilts Herald 27.10.1944, p.5 (photo)
Evening Advertiser 23.10.1944, p.4 (photo)

WEBBER
ERIC
KINGS ROYAL RIFLE CORPS
- Rifleman
- Attended Clarence Street School, Swindon

Source: *North Wilts Herald* 05.11.1943, p.5 (photo)
Evening Advertiser 02.11.1943, p.3 (photo)

WEBBER
MERVYN
DEVONSHIRE REGIMENT
- Private
- Age: 21
- Died: 05.03.1945

Source: *North Wilts Herald* 02.02.1945, p.5
North Wilts Herald 26.01.1945, p.8 (photo)

WEBSTER
LESLIE THOMPSON
ROYAL AIR FORCE Voluntary
- Flight Sergeant
- Age: 33
- Died: 09.10.1944

Source: CWGC

WESTON
ERNEST JAMES
SOMERSET LIGHT INFANTRY
- Private
- Age: 22
- Died: 08.03.1942

Source: CWGC

WHALE
NORMAN MICHAEL
ROYAL NAVY (HMS Glengyle)
- Blacksmith 5th class
- Age: 21
- Died: 11.01.1941

Source: CWGC

WHEELER
ALEXANDER VICTOR (ALEC)
Royal Marine Commandos
- Marine
- Age: 19
- Died: 11.06.1944
- Attended Sanford Street School, Swindon

Source: *North Wilts Herald* 23.06.1944, p.2
Evening Advertiser 22.06.1944, p.1
Evening Advertiser 11.06.1945, p.2

WHISKIN
FREDERICK PERCY
ESSEX REGIMENT
- Private
- Age: 24
- Died: 26.11.1941

Source: CWGC

WHITE
A.
- Private
- From Stratton
- Letter to his fiancée published in *Evening Advertiser*

Source: *Evening Advertiser* 29.08.1944, p.5

WHITE
PERCY VINCENT
ROYAL ARTILLERY
- Gunner/Bombardier
- Age: 23
- Died: 16.08.1944
- Attended Jennings Street School, Swindon

Source: *Great Western Railway Magazine* November 1944, p.175
St Augustine Church Memorial
15 Shop Memorial, STEAM, Swindon
North Wilts Herald 25.08.1944, p.8 (photo)
Evening Advertiser 22.08.1944, p.8 (photo)

WHITEFIELD
LEONARD GEORGE
ROYAL NAVY (HMS Greyhound)
- Petty Officer
- Age: 31
- Died: 22.05.1941

Source: CWGC

WHITEHEAD
EDWARD GEORGE
ROYAL AIR FORCE Voluntary Reserve
- Sergeant Wireless Operator/Air Gunner
- Age: 20
- Died: 27.06.1941

Source: *North Wilts Herald* 06.02.1942, p.5 (photo)
Evening Advertiser 04.07.1941, p.2 (photo)
Evening Advertiser 06.02.1942, p.3 (photo)
Evening Advertiser 27.06.1945, p.2

WHITFIELD
JAMES EDWARD
HOME GUARD
- Age: 39
- Died: 29.06.1941
- Brother of **SIDNEY WHITFIELD**, see below
- Injured in Home Guard practice and died in GWR Medical Fund Hospital
- Buried in Lower Stratton Cemetery

Source: *North Wilts Herald* 22.08.1941, p.3 (photo)
Evening Advertiser 16.08.1941, p.3 (photo)

WHITFIELD SIDNEY
PIONEER CORPS
- Private
- Age: 27
- Died: 11.08.40
- Brother of **JAMES WHITFIELD**, see above
- Died in a military hospital of blood poisoning through his army boots rubbing his heel
- Buried in Lower Stratton Cemetery

Source: *Great Western Railway Magazine* January 1941, p.25
North Wilts Herald 22.11.1940, p.3 (photo)
Evening Advertiser 16.08.1940, p.4 (funeral)
Evening Advertiser 16.08.1941 p.3 (photo)

WIBLING CHARLES WILLIAM
ROYAL ARTILLERY
- Gunner
- Age: 22
- Died: 22.09.1943
- Died in Japanese prisoner of war camp

Source: *Evening Advertiser* 22.07.1943, p.5 (photo)
Evening Advertiser 16.01.1945, p.2
See Prisoners of War

WILLCOCKS CHARLES
ROYAL NAVY
- Chief Petty Officer
- The family was informed that he was 'Missing presumed killed'
- Attended Ferndale Road School, Swindon

Source: *North Wilts Herald* 29.12.1944, p.5 (photo)
Evening Advertiser 23.12.1944, p.8 (photo)

WILLIAMS GEORGE MAURICE
BORDER REGIMENT 1st Airborne Battalion
- Lance Corporal
- Age: 33
- Died: 20.09.1944
- Killed near Nijmegen

Source: CWGC

WILLIAMS ROWLAND ARTHUR
ROYAL AIR FORCE
- Sergeant
- Age: 20
- Died: 23.09.1943
- Attended Sanford Street School, Swindon

Source: *North Wilts Herald* 10.12.1943, p.4 (photo)
Evening Advertiser 01.10.1943, p.2
Evening Advertiser 02.10.1943, p.8 (photo)
Evening Advertiser 15.04.1944, p.2
www.ww2talk.com

WILLIS
JOHN VICTOR WILLIAM
SHERWOOD FORESTERS
- Private
- Age: 25
- Died: 30.08.1944
- Attended Sanford Street School, Swindon

Source: *North Wilts Herald* 28.01.1944, p.3 (photo)
Evening Advertiser 16.09.1944, pp.2/5
Wroughton History Group - Book 10 (2016), p.79

WILMINGTON
FREDERICK HUBERT
ROYAL NAVY (Royal Oak)
- Stoker 1st class
- Age: 29
- Died: 14.10.1939
- Attended Chiseldon School

Source: *Evening Advertiser* 17.10.1939, p.1 (photo)
Evening Advertiser 19.10.1939, p.2

WILSON
ALAN GEORGE RICHARD
ROYAL ARTILLERY 220 Battery
- Gunner
- Age: 22
- Died: 10.07.1944
- Attended Ferndale Road School
- Also known as George Richard Wilson

Source: *Great Western Railway Magazine* September 1944, p.143
15 Shop Memorial, STEAM, Swindon
North Wilts Herald 04.08.44, p.8 (photo)
Evening Advertiser 29.07.1944, pp.2/8 (photo)
Evening Advertiser 10.07.45, p.2

WILSON
CLIFFORD
KINGS OWN SCOTTISH BORDERERS (7th Airborne)
- Sergeant
- Age: 28
- Died: 23.09.1944
- Killed at Arnhem

Source: CWGC

WILSON
ROBERT
RIFLE BRIDGADE
- Rifleman
- Age: 26
- Died: 02.11.1943
- Presumed killed between 2nd-3rd November 1942
- Attended King William Street School, Swindon

Source: *North Wilts Herald* 15.09.1944, p.8 (photo)
Evening Advertiser 26.01.1944, p.3 (photo)

**WIRDHAM
GEOFFREY BADEN**
ROYAL MARINE COMMANDOS
- Marine
- Age: 20
- Died: 05.09.1943
- Drowned in India

Source: *Evening Advertiser* 07.09.1943, p.4 (photo)

**WISE
GEORGE SIDNEY**
ROYAL AIR FORCE Voluntary Reserve
- Corporal
- Age: 42
- Died: 11.03.1943

Source: CWGC

**WISE
JOSEPH RONALD**
ROYAL AIR FORCE Voluntary Reserve
- Sergeant Air Gunner
- Died: 22.02.1945
- Brother of **MAURICE WISE**, see below

Source: *Wroughton History Group - Book 10* (2016), p.79

**WISE
MAURICE THOMAS**
ROYAL ENGINEERS
- Sapper
- Age: 25
- Died: 20.12.1944
- Brother of **JOSEPH WISE**, see above

Source: *Great Western Railway Magazine* February 1945, p.32, Wroughton War Memorial
Wroughton History Group - Book 10 (2016), p.79

**WOOD
FRANCIS ALLEN DUDLEY**
ROYAL ARTILLERY
Lance bombardier
- Age: 22
- Died: 14.10.1940

Source: CWGC

**WOODBRIDGE
WILLIAM HENRY (BILL)**
RECONNAISSANCE CORPS
- Lieutenant
- Age: 28
- Died: 22.06.1944
- Died of wounds received in France
- Attended Euclid Street School, Swindon

Source: *North Wilts Herald* 30.06.1944, p.3 (photo)
Evening Advertiser 28.0.1944, p.5 (photo)
www.highworthhistoricalsociety.co.uk
The Euclidean Christmas 1944 p.3
Evening Advertiser 22.06.1945, p.2
Headlandian Summer 1946, p.30
Highworth War Memorial

**WOODROUGH
ARTHUR THOMAS**
ROYAL NAVY (HMS Ibis)
- Ordinary Telegraphist
- Age: 19
- Died: 10.11.1942

Source: CWGC

WOODWARD
OLIVER LLOYD JONES
ROYAL ARMOURED CORPS
- Trooper
- Age: 21
- Died: 20.05.1941
- Parents lived in Bishopstone

Source: *Evening Advertiser*
20.05.1944, p.2
Bishopstone War Memorial

WOODWARD
STANLEY JAMES
WILTSHIRE REGIMENT
- Private
- Age: 27
- Died: 08.05.1942
- Drowned in India "following an accident while on a bathing parade"
- Attended Sanford Street School, Swindon

Source: *North Wilts Herald*
06.10.1944, p.8 (photo)
Evening Advertiser 22.06.1942, p.1 (photo)
Evening Advertiser 08.05.1943, p.2
Evening Advertiser 10.05.1945, p.2

WOOF
LEONARD FRANK JACKSON
SOMERSET LIGHT INFANTRY
- Private
- Age: 20
- Died: 09.08.1944

Source: *North Wilts Herald*
15.09.1944, p.5 (photo)
Evening Advertiser 24.08.1944, p.8 (photo)
Evening Advertiser 24.08.1944, p.8 (photo)
Evening Advertiser 09.08.1945, p.2

WOOTTON
STANLEY
OXFORDSHIRE AND BUCKINGHAMSHIRE LIGHT INFANTRY
- Private
- Age: 20
- Died: between 10.05.1940 - 04.06.1940

Source: CWGC

WRIGHT
WILLIAM NORMAN
ROYAL NAVY (HMS Mahratta)
- Gunner
- Age: 35
- Died: 25.02.1944

Source: CWGC

PRISONERS OF WAR

ADAMS
HARRY (HAPPY) F.
ROYAL MARINES
- Marine
- Where held: Germany

Source: *Evening Advertiser*
12.02.1944, p.3 (photo),
Evening Advertiser 11.07.1945, p.2
North Wilts Herald 18.02.1944, p.5
(photo)
Great Western Railway Magazine
February 1942, p.45
Great Western Railway Magazine July
1945, p117

ADAMS
JAMES
ROYAL ARTILLERY
- Gunner
- Where held: Japan
- Reported missing early 1942

Source: *Evening Advertiser*
20.07.1943, p.2
Evening Advertiser 21.07.1943, p.2
(photo)

ALLEN
JOHN HERBERT
OX & BUCKS LIGHT INFANTRY
- Sergeant
- Where held: Stalag 383, Germany

Source: *Evening Advertiser*
30.08.2010, p.16
Evening Advertiser 10.09.1940, p.2
(photo)
Evening Advertiser 28.08.1943, p.2
(photo)
Evening Advertiser 08.01.1944, p.5
(photo)

ARNOLD
LESLIE NORMAN
ROYAL ARMY SERVICE CORPS
- Driver
- Where held: Italy and Stalag VIII

Source: *North Wilts Herald*
18.05.1945, p.4 (photo)
Evening Advertiser 29.10.1941, p.2
(photo)
Evening Advertiser 11.05.1945, p.8
Evening Advertiser 11.07.1945, p.2
Great Western Railway Magazine July
1945, p.117

AYRES
HAROLD
ROYAL NORFOLK REGIMENT
- Corporal
- Reported missing after the fall of Singapore

Source: *Evening Advertiser* 17.08.1943, p.2 (photo)

BALCHIN
RICHARD
KINGS ROYAL RIFLES
- Sergeant
- Where held: Stalag VIIIB
- POW No. 4522
- Service No 6844894

Source: *Evening Advertiser* 23.08.1940, p.4
Evening Advertiser 26.03.1943, p.4 (photo)
North Wilts Herald 02.04.1943, p.5 (photo)

BALL
GEORGE HENRY
ROYAL WARWICKSHIRE REGIMENT
- Corporal

Source: *Evening Advertiser* 19.07.2010, p.16
Evening Advertiser 24.07.1940, p.4 (photo)

BARKER
ARTHUR J.
ROYAL ARTILLERY
- Bombardier
- Where held: Germany

Source: *Evening Advertiser* 19.07.2010, p.16
Evening Advertiser 23.07.1940, p.1 (photo)

BARKHAM
FREDERICK SPENCER
ROYAL MARINES
- Gunner
- Where held: Italy
- Captured in Libya, escaped from Italian POW camp to Switzerland.
- Brother **DOUGLAS BARKHAM** was killed in action (see Roll of Honour).
- Attended Gorse Hill School, Swindon

Source: *Evening Advertiser* 28.09.1942, p.4;
Evening Advertiser 16.10.1943, p.5 (photo)

BARRATT
KENNETH
ROYAL ARTILLERY
- Gunner
- Where held: Stalag VIIIB
- Attended Clifton Street School, Swindon

Source: *Evening Advertiser* 30.08.2010, p.16
North Wilts Herald 23.03.1945, p.5
Evening Advertiser 03.09.1940, p.2
Wroughton History Group Book 10, p.90

BARRETT DSC
DENNIS HUGH BRYAN
ROYAL NAVY
- Lieutenant Commander
- Where held: Marlag O Naval camp, Germany
- Captured when HMS Shark was sunk of Norwegian coast.
- Awarded DSC Aug 1945.
- Lived at Wroughton Hall, Wroughton

Source:*Evening Advertiser* 02.08.2010, p.22
Evening Advertiser 08.08.1940, p.4
Evening Advertiser 16.05.1945, p.2 (photo)
Evening Advertiser 19.06.1945, p.5 (photo)
Evening Advertiser 18.09.1945, p.2
Wroughton History Group – Book 7 (1997), p.8
Wroughton History Group - Book - 8 (2002), p.8
Wroughton History Group – Book 9 (2009), p.42-3,
Wroughton History Group - Book 10 (2016), p.147
See Awards & Medals

BERRY
P.
ROYAL NAVY
- Engineroom Artificer

Source: *Great Western Railway Magazine* May 1943, p.76
Great Western Railway Magazine November 1945, p.184

BEWLEY
EDWARD WILLIAM CARPENTER (TED)
ROYAL AIR FORCE
- Flight Sergeant
- Where held: Java
- Died in camp

Evening Advertiser 29.05.1944, p.2
See Roll of Honour

BISHOP
FRANCIS
ROYAL ENGINEERS
- Sapper
- Where held: Italy
- POW in Italy 1942-Aug 1943, then transferred to Germany

Source: *North Wilts Herald* 09.10.1942, p.4 (photo)
Evening Advertiser 08.10.1942, p.4 (photo)
Evening Advertiser 04.09.1943, p.3

BLACKLOCK
WILLIAM
- Lance Corporal
- Where held: Italy then Stalag IVB

Source: *Evening Advertiser* 16.09.1942, p.1 (photo)
Evening Advertiser 01.06.1945, p.5

BOND
E.
ROYAL NORFOLK REGIMENT
- Private
- Where held: Japan
- Attended Jennings Street School, Swindon

Source: *North Wilts Herald* 16.07.1943, p.8 (photo)
Evening Advertiser 17.07.1943, p.2 (photo)

BOWD
BERNARD
- Lance Corporal
- Where held: Stalag VIIIB & XVIIA

Source: *Evening Advertiser*
28.12.1944, p.8
Evening Advertiser 19.05.1945, p.2 (photo)

BOWDEN
A.
ROYAL ENGINEERS
- Sapper

Source: *Great Western Railway Magazine* September 1941, p.240

BOWELL
TERENCE G.W.
ROYAL NAVY
- Stoker
- Where held: Malaya
- Reported missing after the fall of Singapore
- Attended Gorse Hill School, Swindon
- Close friend in camp of POW **JACK SCUTTS**, see below

Source: *North Wilts Herald*
22.04.1943, p.5 (photo)
North Wilts Herald 15.09.1944, p.5 (photo)
Evening Advertiser 08.09.1944, p.5 (photo)
Evening Advertiser 19.4.1943, p.8 (photo)
Evening Advertiser 16.09.1944, p.3
Great Western Railway Magazine December 1943, p.189
Great Western Railway Magazine November 1945, p.184

BOWEN
THOMAS
ROYAL ELECTRICAL AND MECHANICAL ENGINEERS
- Craftsman
- Where held: Japan

Source: *North Wilts Herald*
30.04.1943, p.4 (photo)
Evening Advertiser 25.04.1943, p.4 (photo)
Evening Advertiser 18.09.1943, p.2

BREWER
FRANK
- 2nd Lieutenant
- Where held: Japan
- Brother of **JOHN BREWER**, see below
- Attended Sanford Street School, Swindon

Source: *North Wilts Herald*
03.09.1943, p.8 (photo)
North Wilts Herald 11.02.1944, p.5 (photo)
Evening Advertiser 27.08.1943, p.4 (photo)
Evening Advertiser 04.09.1943, p.3
Evening Advertiser 04.02.1944, p.1 (photo

PRISONERS OF WAR

BREWER (MiD)
JOHN ARTHUR
Major
- Where held: Italy and Germany
- Escaped from Italian camp, recaptured by Germans
- Brother of **FRANK BREWER** see above

Source: *North Wilts Herald* 17.07.1942, p.4 (photo)
North Wilts Herald 03.09.1943, p.8 (photo)
North Wilts Herald 11.02.1944, p.5 (photo)
Evening Advertiser 18.07.1942, p.1 (photo)
Evening Advertiser 27.08.1943, p.4 (photo)
Evening Advertiser 04.09.1943, p.3
Evening Advertiser 04.02.1944, p.1 (photo)
See Awards and Medals

BRIGHT
W.
ROYAL ENGINEERS
- Sergeant
- Where held: Stalag IIIB
- Captured at Dunkirk

Source: *Evening Advertiser* 11.04.1942, p.3 (photo)

BROCK
REGINALD FRANK
ROYAL ARTILLERY
- Gunner
- Where held: Singapore and Sumatra

Source: www.highworthhistoricalsociety.co.uk

BROOKER
CLIFFORD SAMUEL
ESSEX REGIMENT
- Where held: Stalag VIIIB
- Captured at Tobruk

Source: *Evening Advertiser* 19.05.1945, p.2

BROWN
A.
- Gunner
- From Purton

Source: *Evening Advertiser* 03.08.1940, p.3

BROWN
ALBERT GEORGE
ROYAL ARMY SERVICE CORPS
- Lance Corporal
- Where held: Japan
- Died while prisoner of war

Attended Highworth School, Highworth
Source: www.highworthhistoricalsociety.co.uk
See Roll of Honour

BUDDING
LESLIE H.
ROYAL CORPS OF SIGNALS (att RAF)
- Signalman
- Where held: Japan
- Reported missing early 1942
- Attended High School Bath Road, Swindon

Source: *Evening Advertiser* 03.07.1943, p.5

**BULLOCK
LESLIE W.**
ROYAL AIR FORCE Voluntary Reserve
- Flight Sergeant
- Where held: Moulmein, Burma
- Captured at fall of Singapore
- Attended Sanford Street School, Swindon

Source: *North Wilts Herald* 13.03.1942, p.4
North Wilts Herald 27.08.1943, p.5 (photo)
Evening Advertiser 25.08.1943, p.3 (photo)

**BURNETT
ERNEST ROY**
DUKE OF CORNWALL'S LIGHT INFANTRY
- Private
- Where held: Stalag VIIA

Source: *Evening Advertiser* 20.12.1944, p.8 (photo)
Evening Advertiser 16.05.1945, p.2 (photo)

**CAMSICK (CANSICK)
DERRICK**
ROYAL ARMY ORDNANCE CORPS
- Sergeant
- Where held: Italy
- Lived at 'Hillside', Belmont Crescent, Swindon
- Attended Commonweal School, Swindon

Source: *The Euclidean* Summer 1943
North Wilts Herald 11.09.1942, p.4
Commonweal School Magazine Summer 1945, p.7
Baptist Tabernacle Magazine June 1945

**CARTER
WILLIAM THOMAS**
ROYAL ARTILLERY
- Lance Bombardier
- Where held: Japan
- Captured at fall of Singapore

Source: *North Wilts Herald* 30.07.1943, p.6 (photo)
Evening Advertiser 24.07.1943, p.2 (photo)

**CASEY
SIDNEY**
ROYAL MARINES
- Marine
- Where held: Muhlberg, Germany

North Wilts Herald 10.10.1941, p.2

**CLOUGH
G.**
- Corporal
- Where held: Offlag IIIC
- Captured at Dunkirk

Source: *Evening Advertiser* 03.03.1943, p.4 (photo)

**CLARK
CHARLES**
- Signalman
- Where held: Malai Camp
- Reported missing in Malaya in October 1941
- Attended Clarence Street School, Swindon

Source: *Evening Advertiser* 06.05.1943, p.4 (photo)

CLARKE
JOHN GREGORY
- Welsh Guards

Source: *Evening Advertiser*
30.08.2010, p.16
Evening Advertiser 09.09.1940, p.2 (photo)

CLARKE
W. A.
ROYAL ARMY MEDICAL CORPS
- Private
- Where held: Germany

Source: *Evening Advertiser*
30.08.2010, p.16
Great Western Railway Magazine October 1940, p.300
Great Western Railway Magazine November 1944, p.176
Evening Advertiser 03.09.1940, p.2

COID
JAMES
IRISH GUARDS
- Corporal
- Where held: Germany

Source: *Evening Advertiser*
12.07.2010, p.17
Evening Advertiser 08.06.1940, p.1
Evening Advertiser 18.07.1940, p.2 (photo)

COLES
CHARLIE
- Sergeant
- Where held: Stalag 344

Source: *Evening Advertiser*
18.02.1944, p.2 (photo)

COLES
FRANK
- Sergeant
- Where held: Stalag VIIIB

Source: *Evening Advertiser*
19.05.1942, p.1

COOK
ALBERT HENRY GEORGE
- Private
- Where held: Stalag 2E

Source: *Evening Advertiser*
12.05.1945, p.5 (photo)

COOPER
A. B.
ROYAL NAVY
- Where held: Germany
- Attended Stratton School

Source: *North Wilts Herald*
14.05.1943, p.4 (photo)
North Wilts Herald 20.04.1945, p.3 (photo)

COOPER
F.
ROYAL NAVY
- Ordinary Seaman

Source: *Great Western Railway Magazine* June 1943, p.92
Great Western Railway Magazine May 1945, p.100

COOPER
WILLIAM
- Lance Corporal
- Where held: Camp 66 PM 3400

Source: *Evening Advertiser*
15.05.1943, p.2

COUSENS
E. W.
CIVILIAN
- Where held: Borneo
- Chartered Accountant in Treasury of Sarawak Government
- Attended Commonweal School, Swindon

Evening Advertiser 13.08.1943, p.2 (photo)

COX
N.
1st Para Brigade, 1st Airborne Division
- Lance Corporal
- Where held: Stalag IVB
- Captured at Arnhem
- Attended Clarence Street School, Swindon

Source: *Evening Advertiser* 29.05.1945, p.2

CROOK
ERNEST
THE ROYAL MARINES
- Corporal
- Where held: Stalag VIIIB

Source: The Swindon Mirror Aug 1946, pp.4-5.
Evening Advertiser 04.08.2011, p.23 (photo)

CROOK
HENRY REGINALD
ROYAL ENGINEERS
- Sapper
- Where held: Italy

North Wilts Herald 27.03.1942, p.5 (photo)
Evening Advertiser 23.03.1942, p.1 (photo)

CROSS
RONALD CECIL
PARACHUTE REGIMENT
- Private
- Where held: Brunswick
- Captured at Arnhem
- Attended Sanford Street School, Swindon

Source: *North Wilts Herald* 27.04.1945, p.5
Evening Advertiser 02.12.1944, p.5 (photo)
Evening Advertiser 16.10.1944 (photo)

CURTIS
EDWARD ALBERT WALTER
ROYAL ARTILLERY
- Gunner
- Where held: Malai Camp
- Missing for 15 months
- Attended Sanford Street School, Swindon

Source: *North Wilts Herald* 07.05.1943, p4 (photo)
Evening Advertiser 03.05.1943, p.2 (photo)
Evening Advertiser 04.05.1943, p.1

DAVIES
THOMAS HENRY
CHESHIRE REGIMENT/ WELCH FUSILIERS
- Corporal
- Lived at Priors Hill, Wroughton

Source: *Evening Advertiser* 01.08.1940, p.1
Evening Advertiser 19.05.1945, p.2 (photo)
Wroughton History Group - Book 10 (2016), p.88

DELLER
VICTOR
ROYAL ELECTRICAL AND
MECHANICAL ENGINEERS
- Lance Corporal
- Where held: Japan
- Captured at the fall of Singapore
- Attended King William Street School, Swindon

Source: *North Wilts Herald* 23.07.1943, p.5 (photo)
Evening Advertiser 20.07.1943
Wroughton History Group – Book 8 (2002), p.8
Wroughton History Group - Book 10 (2016), p. 88
Evening Advertiser 20.07.1943, p.5

DIXON
FREDERICK
ROYAL NAVY
- Leading Cook
- Where held: Japan
- Missing for 14 months
- A Canadian, who married a woman from Clifton Street

Source: *North Wilts Herald* 18.06.1943, p.5 (photo)
North Wilts Herald 21.05.1943, p.5 (photo)
Evening Advertiser 14.05.1943, p.8 (photo)
Evening Advertiser 12.06.1943, p.2

DIXON
LEONARD GEORGE
QUEEN'S ROYAL REGIMENT
- Where held: Germany Camp 20a Thorn Podgorz
- POW British Army (6456553000)
- Attended High School, Bath Road, Swindon

Source: *Evening Advertiser* 11.09.1940, p.1
Evening Advertiser 12.09.1940, p.1 (photo)

DOBSON
JOHN A.
ROYAL AIR FORCE
- Sergeant Observer
- Where held: Germany
- Attended Euclid Street School, Swindon

Source: *The Euclidean* Summer 1944
Evening Advertiser 31.12.1943, p.5 (photo)

DOWDESWELL
MAURICE
ROYAL AIR FORCE
- Shot down over Europe whilst on an RAF Pathfinder mission

Source: *Wroughton History Group* - Book 7 (1997), p.8

DOWDESWELL
PHILLIP
ROYAL AIR FORCE Voluntary Reserve
- Sergeant Wireless Operator

Source: *Evening Advertiser* 09.11.1944, p.2
Wroughton History Group - Book 10 (2016), p.90

EARLY
JIM
- Where held: Japan

Source: *Wroughton History Group - Book 8* (2002), p.8
Wroughton History Group - Book 10 (2016), p.90

EDMONDS
GEORGE HENRY
OXFORDSHIRE & BUCKINGHAMSHIRE LIGHT INFANTRY
- Private
- Where held: Stalag VIIIB and 344
- Taken prisoner at Dunkirk, released by Russians April 1945
- Attended Westcott Road School, Swindon

Source: *Evening Advertiser* 30.08.2010, p.16
North Wilts Herald 20.04.1945, p.8
Evening Advertiser 09.09.1940, p.2 (photo)
Evening Advertiser 16.04.1945 p.2 (photo)

EDWARDS
TUDOR
- Driver
- Where held: Germany

Source: *Evening Advertiser* 01.07.1940, p.3

EPHGRAVE
GEORGE ARTHUR
ROYAL MARINES
- Marine
- Where held: Germany
- Former Swindon Town goalkeeper

Source: *North Wilts Herald* 15.08.1941, p.8 (photo)
Evening Advertiser 09.08.1941, p.1 (photo)

FALCUS
SEPTIMUS
NORTHUMBERLAND FUSILIERS
- Sergeant
- Where held: Japan

Source: *North Wilts Herald* 02.07.1943, p.4

FORD
E. C.
ROYAL ARTILLERY
- Regimental Sergeant Major
- Where held: Japan
- Captured at fall of Hong Kong, wife was with him in Hong Kong and escaped to Australia

Source: *North Wilts Herald* 10.09.1943, p.6
Evening Advertiser 11.09.1943, p.2

FORD
JESSE
1st AIRBORNE DIVISION
- Lance Corporal
- Where held: Germany

Source: *North Wilts Herald* 22.12.1944, p.4
Evening Advertiser 13.10.1944, p.5 (photo)
Evening Advertiser 20.12.1944, p.4

FOSTER
HENRY
- Where held: Changi
- Was working as a foreman boiler inspector in Singapore before the Japanese invasion
- Lived in Clifton Street, Swindon

Source: *North Wilts Herald* 18.06.1943, p.6
Evening Advertiser 16.06.1943

FRANKLIN
WILLIAM CYRIL
ROYAL BERKSHIRE REGIMENT
Source: *Evening Advertiser* 14.08.1940, p.3

GARNHAM
EDDIE G.
SUFFOLK REGIMENT
- Private
- Where held: Stalag VIIIB
- Spent 6 years as a prisoner of war

Source: *Evening Advertiser* 30.08.2010, p.16.
Evening Advertiser 03.09.1940, p.2
Evening Advertiser 18.05.1945, p.2

GARNHAM
K. W.
ROYAL AIR FORCE
- Leading Aircraftman
- Where held: Greece
- Held by ELAS forces, Greek Communist military wing

Source: *North Wilts Herald* 16.03.1945, p.4 (photo)

GEE
MERVYN JOHN
ROYAL ARTILLERY
- Private
- Where held: Stalag XXA
- *Wroughton History Group* Book 10, p.88
- Captured at Dunkirk

Source: *Evening Advertiser* 22.08.1942, p.4

GEORGE
BASIL
ROYAL ARTILLERY
- Gunner
- Where held: Italy

Source: *Evening Advertiser* 12.08.1942, p.1 (photos)

GITTINGS
FRANCIS EDWARD
SUFFOLK REGIMENT
- Private
- Where held: Malaya
- Missing for 15 months

Source: *Evening Advertiser* 04.05.1943, p.1 (photo)

GORTON/GORDON
H. G.
- Where held: Changi
- Prison Officer in Changi prison, captured at the fall of Singapore. *Evening Advertiser* lists him as Gordon
- Attended Gorse Hill School, Swindon

Source: *North Wilts Herald* 11.06.1943, p.5 (photo)
Evening Advertiser 05.06.1943, p.5 (photo)

GOUGH
FREDERICK (JOCK) WILLIAM
ROYAL ARMY ORDNANCE CORPS/REME
- Quartermaster Sergeant
- Where held: Fukuoka Camp, Japan

Source: *Great Western Railway Magazine* June 1943, p.92
Great Western Railway Magazine December 1945, p.200
North Wilts Herald 16.04.1943, p.5
Evening Advertiser 14.04.1943, p.3

GOUGH
ERIC WILLIAM
ROYAL ARMY ORDNANCE CORPS
- Private
- Where held: Thailand
- Died: 12.10.1943
- Missing for 14 months

Evening Advertiser 13.05.1943, p.3 (photo)
North Wilts Herald 14.05.1943, p.3 (photo)
see Roll of Honour

GREGORY
NORMAN J.
ROYAL AIR FORCE
Sergeant Pilot
- Where held: Stalag IXC 3 & 6
- Reported missing after a night raid on Hamburg
- Attended Euclid Street School, Swindon

Source:*North Wilts Herald* 25.07.1941, p.2 (photo)
Evening Advertiser 30.06.1941, p.1 (photo)
Evening Advertiser 21.07.1941, p.2 (photo)
Evening Advertiser 12.06.1945, p.5
Headlandian Summer 1945, p.22

HACKER
DOUGLAS
- Where held: Germany
- Attended Jennings Street School, Swindon

Source: *North Wilts Herald* 18.02.1944, p.8
Evening Advertiser 17.02.1944, p.2 (photo)

HANCOCK
ROBERT CHARLES
ROYAL AIR FORCE
- Warrant Officer
- Where held: Stalag Luft VI
- Attended Euclid Street School, Swindon

Source: *North Wilts Herald* 20.03.1942, p.8 (photo)
North Wilts Herald 02.03.1945, p.6 (photo)
Evening Advertiser 16.03.1942, p.1 (photo)
The Euclidean Summer 1942
Headlandian Summer 1945, p.22

HATHERALL
JACK
ROYAL NAVY (HMS Repulse)
- Marine
- Where held: Japan
- Picked up by Japanese after sinking of HMS Repulse

Source: *North Wilts Herald* 03.09.1943, p.8 (photo)
Evening Advertiser 28.08.1943, p.2 (photo)

HAYES
FRED (BILL)
ROYAL ARTILLERY
- Lieutenant Quartermaster
- Where held: Japan
- Captured at fall of Singapore

Source: *North Wilts Herald* 04.12.1942, p.5 (photo)
Evening Advertiser 27.12.1942, p.5 (photo)

HAYNES
DONALD
ROYAL ARMY ORDNANCE CORPS
- Private
- Where held: Middle East
- Reported missing June 1942

Source: *North Wilts Herald* 04.09.1942, p4 (photo)
Evening Advertiser 29.08.1942, p.1 (photo)

HAYWARD
W.
ROYAL ENGINEERS
- Sapper
- Where held: Malaya
- Captured at fall of Singapore and escaped from camp
- Attended Sanford Street School, Swindon

Source: *North Wilts Herald* 22.12.1944, p.8 (photo)
Evening Advertiser 20.12.1944, p.2 (photo)

HAZELL
G. O.
ROYAL ARTILLERY
- Gunner
- Where held: Java
- Reported missing February 1942

Source: *Evening Advertiser* 05.07.1943, p.2 (photo)
Evening Advertiser 06.01.1944, p.5 (photo)
North Wilts Herald 09.07.1943, p.4

HAZELL
NORMAN ALEC (LOFTY)
DRAGOON GUARDS
- Trooper
- Where held: Stalag XXIB
- Captured on 14.05.1940

Source: *Evening Advertiser* 20.01.1942, p.2
Evening Advertiser 12.02.1944, p.3 (photo)
North Wilts Herald 18.02.1944, p.5 (photo)
North Wilts Herald 07.01.1944, p.6 (photo)

HERRING
RONALD
ROYAL AIR FORCE
- Aircraftman
- Where held: Java
- Parents ran the Wheatsheaf in Stratton St Margaret

Source: *North Wilts Herald* 09.07.1943, p.5
North Wilts Herald 07.01.1944, p.5
Evening Advertiser 04.01.1944, p.4 (photo)

HICKS
PETER
ROYAL AIR FORCE
- Flight Engineer
- Where held: Germany
- Only survivor of 6 man Lancaster crew, bailed out over north Germany after raid on Stettin

Source: www.highworthhistoricalsociety.co.uk

HILL
JACK ALFRED
ROYAL NAVY
- Marine
- Where held: Japan
- Survivor of HMS Prince of Wales, sunk in December 1941

Source: *North Wilts Herald* 07.07.1944, p.8
North Wilts Herald 17.08.1945, p.4 (photo)
Evening Advertiser 08.07.44, p.1944

HILL
JACK
ROYAL ARMY SERVICE CORPS
- Sergeant
- Where held: Italy/Germany

Source: www.highworthhistoricalsociety.co.uk

HOBBS
STANLEY EDWARD
WILTSHIRE REGIMENT
- Private
- Where held: Stalag VIIIB/IXC & Poland
- Captured in France 22.05.1940

Source: *Evening Advertiser* 12.11.1943, p.4

HOLLAND
RUSSELL DAVID
ROYAL AIR FORCE
- Flying Officer/Flight Lieutenant
- Where held: Stalag Luft 1
- Attended Commonweal School, Swindon

Source: *Evening Advertiser* 11.08.1944, p.2 (photo)
Commonweal School Magazine Summer 1944, p.6
Evening Advertiser 28.06.1945, p.8 (photo)
Evening Advertiser 11.07.1945, p.4
Great Western Railway Magazine August 1944, p.127
Great Western Railway Magazine July 1945, p117

HOLLOWAY
MAURICE
ROYAL AIR FORCE
- Where held: Dulag Luft
- Attended High School, Bath Road, Swindon

Source: *North Wilts Herald* 16.03.1945, p.3
Evening Advertiser 05.07.1944, p.2 (photo)
Evening Advertiser 02.08.1944, p.4 (photo)

HOOPER
JOHN
- Rifleman

Source: *Evening Advertiser* 02.08.2010, p.22
North Wilts Herald 09.08.1940, p.4
North Wilts Herald 08.01.1943, p.4
Evening Advertiser 05.08.1940, p.1

HUGHES
DAI
ROYAL NAVY (HMS Manchester)
- Able Seaman
- Where held: Algiers
- Captured when HMS Manchester was torpedoed

Source: *North Wilts Herald* 11.09.1942, p.4 (photo)

HUMPHRIES
ARTHUR FRANK
ROYAL ENGINEERS
Lance Corporal
- Where held: Stalag VIIIB
- Taken prisoner in Crete
- Attended the College, Swindon

Source: *Great Western Railway Magazine* September 1941, p.240
North Wilts Herald 01.08.1941, p.5
North Wilts Herald 16.06.1942, p.7 (photo)
Evening Advertiser 28.07.1941, p.1 (photo)
Evening Advertiser 10.06.1942, p.2 (photo)
Evening Advertiser 11.07.1945, p.2
Great Western Railway Magazine July 1945, p117

HUNTLEY
JOHN
PARACHUTE REGIMENT
- Private
- Where held: Germany
- Captured at Arnhem
- Attended Clarence Street School, Swindon

Source: *North Wilts Herald* 24.11.44, p.5 (photo)
Evening Advertiser 21.11.1944, p.4 (photo)
Evening Advertiser 04.06.1945, p.2

IRESON
WILLIAM (BILL)
Private
- Where held: Japan
- Captured at fall of Singapore
- Attended Wroughton School

Source: *Wroughton History Group - Book 7* (1997), p.8,
Wroughton History Group - Book 10 (2016), p.89
Evening Advertiser 14.07.1943, p.8 (photo)

ISAAC
JOHN A.
ROYAL AIR FORCE
- Leading Aircraftman
- Where held: Java
- Died in prisoner of war camp

Source: *North Wilts Herald* 03.12.1943, p.3 (photo)
North Wilts Herald 04.06.1943, p.4 (photo)
Evening Advertiser 03.06.1943, p.8 (photo)
Evening Advertiser 30.11.1943, pp.2 & 5 (photo)
See Roll of Honour

JEFFERIES
FRANK
- Private
- Where held: Germany
- Lived in Pinehurst Road, Swindon

Source: *Evening Advertiser* 30.08.2010, p.16
Evening Advertiser 05.09.1940 p.2
Evening Advertiser 30.05.1945, p.2

JENNINGS
ERNEST
MIDDLESEX REGIMENT
- Private
- Where held: Hong Kong

Source: *North Wilts Herald* 14.08.1942, p.8 (photo)

JENNINGS
REGINALD E.
- Signalman
- Where held: Thailand
- Attended Westcott Place School, Swindon
- Captured at the fall of Singapore
- Died from malaria while a prisoner

Source: *North Wilts Herald* 23.07.1943, p.5 (photo)
Evening Advertiser 16.07.1943, p.6 (photo)
Evening Advertiser 27.09.1943, p.8 (photo)
See Roll of Honour

JOHNSTON
HENRY LOUIS
ROYAL ARMY MEDICAL CORPS
- Private
- Where held: Malai Camp
- Missing for 15 months
- From Darlington, he married a woman from Chiseldon who he met at Chiseldon Camp before the war

Source: *North Wilts Herald* 21.05.1943, p.5 (photo)
Evening Advertiser 20.05.1943, p.4 (photo)

JONES
F. J.
GLOUCESTERSHIRE
REGIMENT
- Lance Corporal

Source: *Great Western Railway Magazine* November 1940, p.324
Great Western Railway Magazine December 1943, p.190

KEENE
FRANK
- Where held: Germany
- Captured at Dunkirk
- Attended Clifton Street School, Swindon

Source: *Evening Advertiser* 10.04.1942, p.1 (photo)

KIFF
RONALD
2nd LOTHIAN & BORDER HORSE
- Corporal
- Where held: Italy & Stalag IVB
- Captured at Thalia, North Africa

Source: *Evening Advertiser* 23.05.1945, p.3 (photo)

KIMBER
MERVYN
ROYAL ARTILLERY
- Gunner
- Where held: Italy
- Attended Even Swindon School Swindon

Source: *Evening Advertiser* 17.10.1942, p.4
Evening Advertiser 05.06.1945, p.2
North Wilts Herald 23.10.1942, p.5 (photo)

KITCHENER
GEORGE
ROYAL (10th) HUSSARS
- Trooper
- Where held: Stalag VIIIB
- Captured 14.06.1940 near Rouen
- In January 1945 embarked on 800 mile forced march
- Daughter Heather born while a prisoner of war

Source: *Evening Advertiser* 30.08.2010, p.16
North Wilts Herald 26.12.1941, p.5 (photo)
North Wilts Herald 18.05.1945, p.8 (photo)
Evening Advertiser 04.09.1940, p.2 (photo)
Evening Advertiser 23.12.1940, p.2
Evening Advertiser 14.05.1945, p.2

LAMUDE
FRANK
ROYAL MARINES
- Marine
- Where held: Germany
- Captured at Crete

Source: *North Wilts Herald* 21.11.1941, p.5 (photo)
Evening Advertiser 17.11.1941, p.1 (photo)
Evening Advertiser 16.05.1945, p.4

LANHAM
DONALD STANLEY
QUEEN'S ROYAL REGIMENT
- Where held: Germany

Source: *North Wilts Herald* 18.08.1944, p.8
Evening Advertiser 11.08.1944, p.1 (photo)

LAW
ALBERT
OXFORSHIRE AND
BUCKINGHAMSHIRE LIGHT
INFANTRY
- Died 16.06.1945

Source: War memorial inside St Mary's Church, Purton
See Roll of Honour

LAWSON
JOHN L.
ROYAL ARTILLERY
- Lieutenant
- Where held: Japan
- Captured at fall of Singapore

Source: *North Wilts Herald* 18.12.1942, p.4 (photo
Evening Advertiser 16.12.1942, p.2 (photo)

LEA
J.T.
ROYAL ARMY MEDICAL CORPS
- Where held: Germany
- Attended Commonweal School, Swindon

Source: *The Euclidean* Summer 1943, p.6
Commonweal School Magazine Summer 1945, p.7

LEE
- Private
- Where held: Stalag XXA Poland

Source: *Evening Advertiser* 02.11.1943, p.4

LEONARD
PERCY H.
WILTSHIRE REGIMENT
- Private
- Where held: Stalag XX A91 & XXA 35
- Lived in Ferndale Road, Swindon

Source: *Evening Advertiser* 06.08.1940, p.1
Evening Advertiser 20.12.1941, p.3
Evening Advertiser 20.02.1943, p.4 (photo)
Evening Advertiser 15.05.1945, p.2

LEVY
JOHN
ROYAL ARMY SERVICE CORPS
- Driver
- Where held: Stalag VIIIB or VIIIC
- Captured at Crete, reported missing 2.06.1941
- Attended Clarence Street School, Swindon

Source: *North Wilts Herald* 12.09.1941, p.4 (photo)
North Wilts Herald 09.07.1942, p.4 (photo)
Evening Advertiser 10.09.1941, p.2 (photo)
Evening Advertiser 5.01.1942, p.2
Evening Advertiser 21.07.1943, p.2 (photo)

LEWIS
NORMAN
- Where held: Stammlager IVD
- Captured at the fall of Crete

Source: *Evening Advertiser* 12.10.1944, p.2 (photo)

LEWIS
TREVOR
ROYAL NAVY (HMS Sikh)
- Chief Petty Officer
- Where held: Italy
- Reported missing following action at Tobruk

Source: *Evening Advertiser* 09.11.1942, p.8

LORD DFC
D. S.
ROYAL AIR FORCE
- Flight Lieutenant

Source: *Evening Advertiser* 22.01.1945, p.3
See Awards and Medals

LOVEDAY
GERALD S.
ROYAL AIR FORCE
- Sergeant
- Where held: Germany
- He was engaged to a woman from Swindon

Source: *Evening Advertiser* 06.04.1943, p.8 (photo)

LOXTON
ALBERT
ROYAL MARINES
- Marine
- Where held: Italy
- Captured at Tobruk
- March 1943 he was exchanged for an Italian prisoner of war

Source: *Evening Advertiser* 26.03.1942, p.1 (photo)
Evening Advertiser 24.06.1943, p.5 (photo)

LUCAS
ALBERT
ROYAL TANK REGIMENT
- Trooper
- Where held: Italy
- Attended Sanford Street School, Swindon

Source: *North Wilts Herald* 11.09.1942, p.4 (photo)

LYFORD
RONALD WILLIAM
ROYAL ARMY ORDNANCE CORPS
- Private
- Where held: Germany

Source: *North Wilts Herald* 22.08.1941, p.4;

MABBERLEY
HENRY JAMES
ROYAL ARTILLERY
- Gunner
- Where held: Italy & Stalag IVF
- Attended King William Street School, Swindon

Source: *Evening Advertiser* 26.03.1942, p.1 (photo)
Evening Advertiser 19.05.1945, p.2

MAGEE
JOHN
ROYAL ARMY MEDICAL CORPS
- Corporal
- Where held: Stalag XXA Poland

Source: *Evening Advertiser* 02.11.1943, p.4 (photo)

MALLER
GERALD ERNEST
- Where held: Germany
- Captured at Dunkirk

Source: *North Wilts Herald* 10.07.1942, p.8 (photo)
Evening Advertiser 06.07.1942, p.3 (photo)

MASON
GEORGE
GREEN HOWARDS
- Private
- Where held: Stalag VIIIB/344 (Poland) & Camp 66 (Italy)
- Captured near Tobruk 1.06.1942
- While a prisoner in Italy, he escaped and was recaptured by Germans

Source: *North Wilts Herald* 20.04.1945
Evening Advertiser 16.04.1945, p.2 (photo)
Evening Advertiser 24.12.1942, p.8

MASTERS
ARTHUR
ROYAL TANK REGIMENT
- Trooper
- Where held: Italy & Germany

Source: *Evening Advertiser* 21.05.1945, p.5 (photo)

MATTHEWS
M. G.
- Royal Corps of Signals
- Where held: Formosa (Taiwan)
- Attended Commonweal School, Swindon

Source: *The Euclidean* Summer 1943, p.6

MATTHEWS
GORDON/GERALD
ROYAL AIR FORCE
- Flying Officer
- Where held: Stalag Luft 1
- *Evening Advertiser* calls him both Gerald and Gordon
- Brother to **DOUGLAS MATTHEWS**, see Roll of Honour

Source: *Evening Advertiser* 18.05.1945, p.2
Evening Advertiser 19.05.1945, p8
Evening Advertiser 28.06.1945, p.8

McMILLAN
ALEXANDER CHARLES
ROYAL AIR FORCE
- Flying Officer
- Where held: Germany

Source: *North Wilts Herald* 30.07.1943, p.4 (photo)
Evening Advertiser 27.07.1943, p.5 (photo)

MEAD
MAURICE
- Captured during the North Africa campaign

Source: *Wroughton History Group - Book 7* (2002), p.8
Wroughton History Group - Book 10 (2016) p.90

MESSENGER
GEORGE
- Private
- Where held: Italy
- Captured in Libya

Source: *North Wilts Herald* 28.08.1942, p.3 (photo)

MILES
F. E. W.
ROYAL ARMY ORDNANCE CORPS
- Private
- Died while a prisoner of war

Source: *Great Western Railway Magazine* December 1943, p.189
Great Western Railway Magazine November 1945, p.184

MILES
HENRY CHARLES
CAMBRIDGESHIRE REGIMENT
- Private
- Where held: Singapore

Source: www.highworthhistoricalsociety.co.uk

MILES
VIVIAN
ROYAL ARTILLERY
- Gunner
- Where held: Stalag IVB
- Captured at Dunkirk

Source: *Evening Advertiser* 26.05.1945, p.5 (photo)

MILLIN
REGINALD GEORGE
- Private
- Where held: Japan
- Reported missing after the fall of Singapore
- Attended Even Swindon School, Swindon
- brother of **VICTOR MILLIN**, see below

Source: *North Wilts Herald* 27.08.1943, p.5 (photo)
North Wilts Herald 07.01.1944
Evening Advertiser 02.04.1942, p.1 (photo)
Evening Advertiser 24.08.1943, p.2 (photo)
Evening Advertiser 04.01.1944, p.2

MILLIN
VICTOR EDWARD
ROYAL ARMY SERVICE CORPS
- Driver
- Where held: Germany/Italy
- Brother of **REGINALD MILLIN**, see above

Source: *Great Western Railway Magazine* November 1942, p.196
North Wilts Herald 07.01.1944, p.5
Evening Advertiser 10.09.1942, p.1
Evening Advertiser 04.01.1944, p.2

MONEY
J.J.
- Captain
- Where held: Germany

Source: *Evening Advertiser* 25.01.1944, p.8
Wroughton History Group - Book 10 (2016), p.89

MOORE
GORDON WELHAM
ROYAL (INDIAN) ARMY ORDNANCE CORPS
- Captain
- Where held: Malaya
- Captured at fall of Singapore
- Attended Commonweal School, Swindon

Source: *The Euclidean* Summer 1943, p.6
Great Western Railway Magazine February 1943, p.29
North Wilts Herald 08.01.1943, p.4 (photo)
Evening Advertiser 04.01.1943, p.4 (photo)
Evening Advertiser 05.06.1943, p.8 (photo);
Great Western Railway Magazine December 1945, p.199

MORGAN
F. R. C.
ROYAL ARMY ORDNANCE CORPS
- Staff Sergeant
- Where held: Italy

Source: *North Wilts Herald* 18.09.1942, p.8 (photo)
Evening Advertiser 15.09.1942, p.2 (photo)

MOSS
TOM A.
ROYAL ENGINEERS
- Sapper
- Where held: Germany
- Died in camp as result of an accident

Source: *Great Western Railway Magazine* December 1941, p.328
Great Western Railway Magazine January 1945, p.15
North Wilts Herald 05.10.1941, p.8
Evening Advertiser 05.02.1942, p.2 (photo)
see Roll of Honour

MUSTO
RONALD
- Paratrooper
- Where held: Stalag IVB
- Captured at Arnhem
- Attended Gorse Hill School, Swindon

Source: *Evening Advertiser* 17.10.1944, p.2
North Wilts Herald 17.11.1944, p.5 (photo)
Evening Advertiser 14.11.1944, p.5
Evening Advertiser 30.05.1945, p.2 (photo)

MUTTER
A. R.
WILTSHIRE REGIMENT
- Lieutenant

Source: *North Wilts Herald* 15.08.1941, p.4

NESBIT
CHARLES
IRISH GUARDS
- Guardsman
- Where held: Middle East
- From Ireland, married a girl from Summers Street, Swindon

Source: *Evening Advertiser* 28.04.1943, p.5 (photo)

NOBES
R. J.
WORCESTERSHIRE REGIMENT
- Private

Source: *Great Western Railway Magazine* Apr 1941, p.112

OBORNE
JACK B.
ROYAL ARTILLERY
- Bombardier
- Captured in Libya

Where held: Italy
Source: *North Wilts Herald* 04.09.1942, p.5
Evening Advertiser 29.08.1942, p.3 (photo)

PAGE
ALBERT JAMES
- Private
- Where held: Germany

Source: *Evening Advertiser* 30.08.2010, p.16
Evening Advertiser 03.09.1940
Evening Advertiser 24.07.1940, p.4 (photo)

PALMER
H. L.
ROYAL ARMY SERVICE CORPS
- Driver
- Where held: Italy and Germany

Source: *Great Western Railway Magazine* April 1943, p.60
Evening Advertiser 23.05.1945, p.4 (photo)
Evening Advertiser 11.07.1945, p.2
Great Western Railway Magazine July 1945, p117

PARKER
HAROLD G.
ROYAL AIR FORCE Medical Corps
- Corporal
- Where held: Java
- Reported missing March 1942

Source: *North Wilts Herald* 16.07.1943, p.5 (photo)
North Wilts Herald 14.07.1944, p.5 (photo)
Evening Advertiser 22.04.1942, p.4 (photo)
Evening Advertiser 13.07.1943, p.2 (photo)
Evening Advertiser 12.07.1944, p.4 (photo)

PAYNE
WALTER GEORGE
- Sergeant
- Where held: Germany

North Wilts Herald 14.04.1944, p.4
Evening Advertiser 10.04.1944, p.4 (photo)

PEARCE
ALBERT GEORGE HENRY
THE LINCOLNSHIRE REGIMENT
- Private
- Where held: Stalag XXB
- Lived in Albion Street, Swindon
- Attended Clifton Street School, Swindon

Source: *Evening Advertiser* 30.08.2010, p.16
Evening Advertiser 07.09.1940 p.3 (photo)
Evening Advertiser 16.12.1943 p.3 (photo)
Evening Advertiser 17.05.1945, p.2

PERRY
GEORGE F.
ROYAL ARMY ORDNANCE CORPS
- Driver
- Where held: Germany

Evening Advertiser 09.09.1940, p.1

PHILLIPS
NORMAN ROBERT
ROYAL ENGINEERS
- Sapper
- Where held: Germany
- Killed in road accident in Sherborne, Dorset within a week of being demobbed
- Buried at Whitworth Road Cemetery, Swindon

Source: *Great Western Railway Magazine* August 1941, p.213
Western Gazette 01.03.1946, p.2

POPE
IVOR AFLECK
ROYAL ARTILLERY HAA
- Gunner
- Where held: Java
- Attended Even Swindon School, Swindon
- Died: 29.11.1943

Source: St Augustine Church Memorial
North Wilts Herald 28.05.1942, p.7
North Wilts Herald 28.01.1944, p.4 (photo)
Evening Advertiser 21.05.1943, p.2 (photo)
Evening Advertiser 27.01.1944, p.1 (photo)
See Roll of Honour

PORTER
EDWARD CHARLES
- Private
- Lived at St. Philips Rd., Upper Stratton

Evening Advertiser 03.08.1940, p.3

POUNDER
GEORGE VERNAL
ROYAL ARTILLERY
- Bombardier
- Where held: Germany
- Lived at Priors Hill, Wroughton
- Captured at Dunkirk

Source: *Evening Advertiser* 02.08.2010, p.22,
Evening Advertiser 08.08.1940, p.2,
Wroughton History Group - Book 7 (1997), p.8
Wroughton History Group - Book 10 (2016), p.90

POWELL
B.
- Gunner
- Where held: Fukuoka Camp
- Attended Lethbridge Road School, Swindon

Source: *North Wilts Herald* 05.01.1945, p.5
Evening Advertiser 01.01.1945, p.3

PULLEN
ARTHUR
ARMY AIR CORPS, 1st Parachute Division
Paratrooper
- Where held: Germany
- Captured at Arnhem
- Attended Lethbridge Road School, Swindon

Source: *North Wilts Herald* 22.12.1944, p.5 (photo)
Evening Advertiser 20.12.1944, p.2 (photo)
Evening Advertiser 02.06.1945, p.8 (photo)

RAWLINSON
GEORGE
ROYAL NAVY (HMS Sikh)
- Petty Officer
- Where held: Italy
- Prisoner exchanged March 1943

Source: *Evening Advertiser* 29.03.1943, p.3 (photo)

RICHARDSON
ALAN
- Where held: Germany

Source: *Baptist Tabernacle Magazine* June 1945

RICHARDSON
F.
OXFORDSHIRE & BUCKINGHAMSHIRE LIGHT INFANTRY
- Private
- Where held: Stalag IVA

Source: *Evening Advertiser* 19.05.1945, p.2

RICHARDSON
W.A.
Commonweal School Mag Summer 1945, p.7

ROGERS
CHARLES HALMA
ROYAL NAVY (HMS Repulse)
- Petty Officer
- Where held: Japan
- Reported missing when HMS Repulse sank Aug 1942

Source: *North Wilts Herald* 27.08.1943, p.5 (photo)
Evening Advertiser 08.1943, p.5 (photo)

ROWLAND
RAYMOND
- Private
- Where held: Thailand
- Reported missing after the fall of Singapore
- Attended King William Street School, Swindon

Source: *North Wilts Herald* 14.05.1943, p.4 (photo)
Evening Advertiser 07.04.1942, P.3
Evening Advertiser 10.05.1943, p.8 (photo)

**SANDALL
W. A.
ESSEX REGIMENT**
- Private

Source: *Great Western Railway Magazine* July 1944, p.110

**SARGENT
BEN
WORCESTERSHIRE REGIMENT**
- Acting Corporal
- Where held: Stalag XXB
- Lived in Omdurman Street, Swindon
- Underwent 900 mile death march

Source: *Evening Advertiser* 06.08.1940, p.1
Evening Advertiser 17.05.1945, p.2 (photo)
Evening Advertiser 11.07.1945, p.2
Great Western Railway Magazine October 1940, p.300
Great Western Railway Magazine July 1945, p117

**SCUTTS
JACK B. (M?)
ROYAL NAVY** (HMS Prince of Wales)
- Stoker
- Where held: Malaya
- Involved in sinking of the Bismarck,
- Missing for 18 months
- Became landlord of The Southbrook, Swindon
- Attended Gorse Hill School, Swindon
- Close friend in POW camp of **TERRY BOWELL**, see above

Source: *Great Western Railway Magazine* December 1943, p.189
North Wilts Herald 04.06.1943, p.5 (photo)
North Wilts Herald 13.04.1945, p 5
Evening Advertiser 31.05.1943, p.5
Evening Advertiser 07.04.1945, p.2 (photo)
Great Western Railway Magazine December 1945, p.199

SELWOOD
HERBERT WALTER JAMES
ROYAL ARTILLERY
- Gunner
- Where held: Thailand and Manila
- Captured at the fall of Singapore
- Released from Bilibid Camp, Manila by Americans but died of malnutrition
- Attended Clarence Street School, Swindon

Source: *North Wilts Herald* 23.07.1943, p.8 (photo)
North Wilts Herald 02.03.1945. p.4 (photo)
Evening Advertiser 20.07.43, p.4 (photo)
North Wilts Herald 23.03.1945, p.8 (photo)
See Roll of Honour

SHORTO
KENNETH
- Signalman
- Where held: Japan

Source: *North Wilts Herald* 04.06.1943, p.4

SHUTTLEWORTH
CHARLES
ROYAL ARTILLERY
- Gunner
- Where held: Italy

Source: *North Wilts Herald* 11.12.1942, p.5
Evening Advertiser 08.12.1942, p5
Wroughton History Group - Book 10 (2016), p.89

SILK
ERNEST
WILTSHIRE REGIMENT
- Private
- Where held: Germany

Source: *Evening Advertiser* 19.07.2010, p.16

SIMPKINS
ALBERT
- Private
- Where held: Italy
- Escaped to Switzerland

Source: *North Wilts Herald* 12.11.1943, p.4 (photo)
Evening Advertiser 02.12.1942, p.4 (photo)
Evening Advertiser 09.11.1943, p.2
Wroughton History Group - Book 10 (2016), p.89

SINNETT
SIDNEY DAVID
- Rifleman
- Where held: Stalag VIIIB and camps in France, Germany and Czechoslovakia
- Lived at 55 Corby Avenue
- Taken prisoner at Calais 07.06.1940

Source: *Evening Advertiser* 16.08.1940, p.2
Evening Advertiser 27.09.1943, p.5 (photo)
Evening Advertiser 06.02.1945, P.2
Evening Advertiser 11.05.1945, p.2 (photo)
Headlandian Summer 1945, p.22

**SLADE
KENNETH JAMES
QUEEN'S OWN ROYAL WEST KENTS**
- Sergeant
- Where held: Stalag VIIA
- Son of Managing Director of Garrard's

Source: *North Wilts Herald* 18.05.1945, p.8 (photo)
Evening Advertiser 01.08.1944, p.2 (photo)
Evening Advertiser 15.09.1944, p.1 (photo)
Evening Advertiser 14.05.1945, p.2

**SMITH
A. T.
ROYAL ELECTRICAL AND MECHANICAL ENGINEERS**
- Craftsman
- Captured at Tobruk

Source: *Evening Advertiser* 01.06.1945, p.2

**SMITH
DONAL E.
ROYAL AIR FORCE**
- Flight Lieutenant
- Where held: Germany

Source: *Evening Advertiser* 01.06.1945, p.2

**SMART
SIDNEY
ROYAL NAVY (HMS Exeter)**
- Able Seaman
- Where held: Japan
- Missing from March 1942

Source: *North Wilts Herald* 04.06.1943, p.8 (photo)
Evening Advertiser 03.06.1943, p.3 (photo)

**SMITH
FRED (BILL)
ROYAL ARMY ORDNANCE CORPS**
- Private
- Where held: Italy
- Missing from June 1942

Source: *North Wilts Herald* 25.09.1942, p.4
Evening Advertiser 18.08.1942, p.1
Evening Advertiser 21.09.1942, p.1 (photo)
Wroughton History Group - Book 10 (2016), p.89

**SMITH
HARRY
ROYAL NORFOLK REGIMENT**
- Private
- Where held: Malai Camp
- Attended Gorse Hill School, Swindon

Source: *North Wilts Herald* 04.06.1943, p.8 (photo)

**SMITH
HARRY THOMAS
ROYAL AIR FORCE**
- Leading Aircraftman
- Where held: Japan
- Missing from December 1941

Source: *North Wilts Herald* 18.06.1943, p.5 (photo)
North Wilts Herald 07.01.1944, p.5
Evening Advertiser 12.06.1943, p.1 (photo)
Evening Advertiser 03.01.1944, p.2 (photo)

SMITH
RAY
- Private
- Where held: Italy

Source: *North Wilts Herald*
18.09.1942, p.5 (photo)
Evening Advertiser 11.09.1942, p.1
(photo)

SMITTEN
HARRY
ROYAL NORFOLK REGIMENT
- Private
- Where held: Malai Camp
- Captured at the fall of Singapore
- Attended Gorse Hill School, Swindon

Source: *North Wilts Herald*
20.08.1943, p.6
Evening Advertiser 02.04.1942, p.4
(photo)
Evening Advertiser 02.06.1943, p.5
(photo)
See Roll of Honour

SPACKMAN
KENNETH
- Sergeant
- Where held: Italy

Source: *Evening Advertiser*
26.08.1942

SPRAGG
LLOYD
Interned Civilian
- Where held: Changi
- Foreman in Federal Malay States Railway, captured at Singapore
- Attended Clifton Street School, Swindon

Source: *Evening Advertiser*
02.06.1943, p.6 (photo)
North Wilts Herald 04.06.1943, p.5
(photo)
Baptist Tabernacle Magazine
November 1945

SPURLOCK
KEN C.
ROYAL CORPS OF SIGNALS
- Lieutenant Signals Officer
- Where held: Japan
- Captured by the Japanese in Burma
- Served as Major General Wingate's Principal Signals Officer
- Attended Swindon Secondary School

Source: *Swindonian* pp.922 & 929
North Wilts Herald March 1944, p.
Evening Advertiser 15.03.1944, p.5
(photo)
Evening Advertiser 19.05.1945, p.8
(photo)
Baptist Tabernacle Magazine
November 1945

STANLEY
A. J. E.
PARACHUTE REGIMENT
- Private
- Where held: Germany
- Captured after Arnhem
- Attended King William Street School, Swindon

Source: *Great Western Railway Magazine* January 1945, p.16
Evening Advertiser 01.12.1944, p.4 (photo)

STANNAWAY
ALBERT EDWARD
ROYAL AIR FORCE Voluntary Reserve
- Aircraftman
- Where held: Japan
- Missing from February 1942

Source: *North Wilts Herald* 11.06.1943, p.4 (photo)
Evening Advertiser 05.06.1943, p.4 (photo)

STARR
JIM
ROYAL TANK REGIMENT
- Trooper
- Where held: Germany and Italy
- Reported missing 17.06.1941 in the Middle East

Source: *North Wilts Herald* 08.08.1941, p.3 (photo)
Evening Advertiser 04.08.1941, p.3 (photo)
Evening Advertiser 01.06.1945, p.4 (photo)
Evening Advertiser 04.08.2011, p.23 (photo)

STONE
ROYAL AIR FORCE
- Leading Aircraftman
- Held by ELAS forces, the Greek People's Liberation Army

Source: *North Wilts Herald* 16.03.1945, p.4 (photo)
North Wilts Herald 23.03.1945, p.3

STRANGE
CECIL
ROYAL WEST KENT REGIMENT
- Private
- Where held: Stalag XXB Marienberg

Source: *North Wilts Herald* 26.05.1944, p.5 (photo)

STRATFORD
L. G.
ROYAL ELECTRICAL AND MECHANICAL ENGINEERS
- Sergeant
- Where held: Japan
- Had a hairdressing business at 198 Rodbourne Road

Source: *North Wilts Herald* 05.03.1943, p.7 (photo)
Evening Advertiser 04.03.1943, p.8 (photo)

SWAIN
ROY
WILTSHIRE REGIMENT
- Private
- Where held: Germany
- Captured at Dunkirk

Source: *North Wilts Herald* 14.08.1942, p.8
Evening Advertiser 17.05.1945, p.2

PRISONERS OF WAR

TAME
ALBERT LIONEL
ROYAL AIR FORCE
- Aircraftman 2nd class
- Where held: Java
- Died in camp
- Attended Highworth School

Source: *North Wilts Herald* 07.01.1944, p.6
www.highworthhistoricalsociety.co.uk
Highworth War Memorial
Evening Advertiser 01.01.1944, p4 (photo)
See Roll of Honour

TAYLER
RON
ROYAL AIR FORCE
- Leading Aircraftman
- Where held: Burma

Source: *North Wilts Herald* 17.08.1945, p.4 (photo)

THOMPSON
- Corporal
- Where held: Stalag XXA Poland

Source: *Evening Advertiser* 02.11.1943, p.4

THOMPSON
JACK B.
SEAFORTH HIGHLANDERS
- Sergeant
- Where held: Germany
- Goalkeeper for Swindon Victoria Football Club

Source: *Great Western Railway Magazine* June 1943, p.92
North Wilts Herald 06.02.1942, p.7
Evening Advertiser 11.07.1945, p.2
Great Western Railway Magazine July 1945, p117

THOMPSON
VERNON
OXFORDSHIRE AND BUCKINGHAMSHIRE LIGHT INFANTRY
- Platoon Sergeant Major
- Where held: Stalag 357
- Lived in Ferndale Road, Swindon
- Captured at Dunkirk

Source: *Evening Advertiser* 21.06.2010, p.18 (photo)
Evening Advertiser 12.07.2010, p.17
Evening Advertiser 18.07.1940, p.1 (photo)
Evening Advertiser 01.09.1940, p.1

TIMMS
F.J.
ROYAL ARMY SERVICE CORPS
- Driver
- Where held: Germany
- Captured at Arnhem

Source: *North Wilts Herald* 01.12.1944, p.8 (photo)
Evening Advertiser 29.11.1944, p.4 (photo)

TITCOMBE
J.R.
- Lance Corporal
- Where held: Italy and Germany

Source: *Evening Advertiser* 30.05.1945, p.2

TOWNSEND
S. J.
ROYAL ARTILLERY
- Gunner
- Where held: Java

Source: *North Wilts Herald* 16.07.1944, p.4 (photo)
Evening Advertiser 10.07.1943, p.5 (photo)

TREASURE
JOHN VICTOR
ROYAL ARTILLERY
- Lieutenant
- Where held: Jinsen, Korea
- Lived in Victoria Road, Swindon
- Reported missing 15.02.1942
- Attended Swindon Secondary School

Source: *The Swindonian* pp.922 & 929
North Wilts Herald 02.04.43, p.3 (photo)
North Wilts Herald 11.06.43, p.5
North Wilts Herald 22.10.1943, p.6 (photo)
North Wilts Herald 17.08.1945, p.4 (photo)
'Millennium Memories' Swindon: ELSP, 2000, p.194
Evening Advertiser 01.04.1943, p.1, (photo)
Evening Advertiser 05.06.1943, p.8
Evening Advertiser 19.10.1943, p.4 (photo)
Evening Advertiser 23.1.1943, p.3

TUCK
J. F.
SUFFOLK REGIMENT
- Private
- Where held: Japan
- Reported missing early 1942

Source: *North Wilts Herald* 16.07.1943, p.8
Evening Advertiser 15.07.1943, p.2
Great Western Railway Magazine November 1945, p.184

TURNER
JOHN E.
ROYAL ARMY ORDNANCE CORPS/REME
- Private/ Craftsman
- Where held: Japan
- Missing from February 1942

Source: *Great Western Railway Magazine* November 1943, p.172
North Wilts Herald 23.07.1943, p.5 (photo)
North Wilts Herald 16.07.1943, p.3 (photo);
Great Western Railway Magazine December 1945, p.199

TUTT
ALFRED RICHARD (RICHARD)
DORSET REGIMENT
- Private
- Where held: Germany
- Attended Purton Church of England School

Source: *North Wilts Herald* 11.08.1944 (photo)
North Wilts Herald 15.09.1944, p.5 (photo)
Evening Advertiser 09.08.1944, p.8 (photo)
Evening Advertiser 12.09.1944, p.4 (photo)
Evening Advertiser 11.07.1945, p.2
Great Western Railway Magazine November 1944, p.175
Great Western Railway Magazine July 1945, p.117

TYLEE
RONALD CHARLES E.
ROYAL AIR FORCE
- Sergeant Pilot
- Where held: Stalag VIIIB
- Undertook a 600 mile march

Source: *Evening Advertiser* 23.05.1945, p.4 (photo)
Evening Advertiser 11.07.1945, p.2
Great Western Railway Magazine April 1943, p.60
Great Western Railway Magazine 1945, pp.100/101

VARNEY
REGINALD
- Gunner
- Where held: Java

Source: *North Wilts Herald* 09.07.1943, p.3 (photo)

VICKERY
DENNIS
- Private
- Where held: Germany
- Lived in King William Street, Swindon
- Captured in Belgium

Source: *Evening Advertiser* 30.08.2010, p.16
Evening Advertiser 05.09.1940, p.2

WAKLEY
A.
ROYAL ARMY ORDNANCE CORPS/REME
- Sergeant
- Where held: Japan
- Missing for 19 months before reported a prisoner
- Attended Sanford Street School, Swindon

Source: *North Wilts Herald* 20.08.1943, p.6 (photo)
Great Western Railway Magazine November 1943, p.172
Great Western Railway Magazine November 1945, p.184

WEBB
ARTHUR STANLEY
ROYAL ARMY MEDICAL CORPS 1st Airborne Division
- Private
- Where held: Stalag IVB
- Captured at Arnhem
- Attended Ferndale Road School, Swindon

Source: *North Wilts Herald* 15.12.1944, p.5 (photo)
Evening Advertiser 12.12.1944, p.8
Evening Advertiser 31.05.1945, p.4 (photo)

WEBB
H. GEORGE
ROYAL MARINES
- Marine
- Where held: Germany
- Missing after Battle of Crete

Source: *Evening Advertiser* 23.01.1942, p.1 (photo)

WEBB
RONNIE J.
ROYAL MARINES
- Marine
- Where held: Germany
- Escaped from camp during Allied advance, walked 600 miles across Germany
- Family information states he was captured during evacuation of Crete and was held in Stalag VIIIB

Source: *North Wilts Herald* 08.08.1941, p.5 (photo)
Evening Advertiser 06.08.1941, p.2 (photo)
Evening Advertiser 12.04.1945, p.8 (photo)
Great Western Railway Magazine May 1945, pp.100/101
Evening Advertiser 04.08.2011, p.23 (photo)

WEBB-MORRIS (MM)
TED
ROYAL TANK REGIMENT
- Regimental Quartermaster Sergeant
- Where held: Libya & Italy
- Captured in Libya, transferred to Italy
- Escaped camp and was sheltered by Italian family while posing as a deaf and mute man
- Attended Lethbridge Road School, Swindon

Source: *North Wilts Herald* 04.09.1942, p4 (photo)
North Wilts Herald 12.05.1944, p.5 (photo)
Evening Advertiser 28.08.1942, p.1 (photo)
Evening Advertiser 24.12.1943, p.1 (photo)
Evening Advertiser 06.05.1944, p.2 (photo)
See Awards and Medals

WESTMACOTT
A. G.
CAMBRIDGESHIRE REGIMENT
- Private
- Where held: Japan
- Reported missing January 1942
- Attended Sanford Street School, Swindon

Source: *North Wilts Herald* 16.07.1943, p.5 (photo)
Evening Advertiser 13.07.1943, p.5 (photo)
Great Western Railway Magazine September 1943, p.140
Great Western Railway Magazine November 1945, p.184

PRISONERS OF WAR

WIBLING
CHARLES
ROYAL ARTILLERY
- Gunner
- Where held: Japan
- Captured at the fall of Singapore
- Died in camp

Source: *Evening Advertiser* 16.01.1945, p.2
Evening Advertiser 22.07.1943, p.5 (photo)
See Roll of Honour

WILLIAMS
EDWIN JOHN
ROYAL ARTILLERY
- Gunner
- Where held: Stalag VIIIB
- Lived in Kingshill Road, Swindon
- Captured in France

Source: *Evening Advertiser* 30.08.2010, p.16
North Wilts Herald 17.09.1943, p.4
Evening Advertiser 06.09.1940 p.2 (photo)
Evening Advertiser 08.07.1942, p.2

WILLIAMS
L.J.
ROYAL AIR FORCE
- Leading Aircraftman

Source: *Great Western Railway Magazine* May 1944, p.82

WILLOUGHBY
HENRY ALFRED
GLOUCESTERSHIRE REGIMENT
- Where held Stalag 8B
- Captured 1st June 1940 at Cassell on the Dunkirk perimeter
- Home address 1 Ermin Street

Source: Family information

WITTS
FREDERICK
- Private
- Where held: Stalag VIIIB

Source: *Evening Advertiser* 12.11.1943, p.4

WOODHOUSE
WILFRED JOHN
SOMERSET LIGHT INFANTRY
- Private
- Where held: Stalag A7 & 344
- Killed in action in Korean War 04.01.1951

Source: *North Wilts Herald* 11.05.1945, p.4
North Wilts Herald 11.05.1945, p.4
Evening Advertiser 10.05.1945, p.2
Evening Advertiser 10.01.1951, pp.1&6
Evening Advertiser 15.01.1951, pp.1&6

WOODWARD
ALBERT EDWARD
ROYAL TANK REGIMENT
- Trooper
- Where held: Italy

Source: *North Wilts Herald* 28.08.1942, p.4 (photo)
Evening Advertiser 25.08.1942, p.3 (photo)

GALLANTRY AWARDS AND MEDALS

**ARKELL
JAMES WILLIAM**
ROYAL GURKHA RIFLES
- Major
- Award: Military Cross and Bar
- "For distinguished and gallant service in Burma"
- Killed in action in Malaya 1946

Source: www.highworthhistoricalsociety.co.uk
Highworth War Memorial
North Wilts Herald 09.07.1943, p.7
North Wilts Herald 17.05.1944, p.4 (photo)
North Wilts Herald 18.08.1944, p.5 (photo)
Evening Advertiser 18.05.1944, pp.2 & 8 (photo)
Evening Advertiser 16.08.1944, p.4 (photo)
See Roll of Honour

**ARNOLD-FORSTER
MARK**
ROYAL NAVY VOLUNTEER RESERVE
- Lieutenant
- Award: Distinguished Service Cross
- Grandson of Mrs H G Arnold-Forster of Bassett Down House

Source: *North Wilts Herald* 19.03.1943, p.4

**ASTLE
ALFRED (FREDDIE)**
ROYAL AIR FORCE Voluntary Reserve
- Pilot Officer
- Award: Distinguished Flying Cross
- Shot down over Germany 24.09.1944

Source: *North Wilts Herald* 03.03.1944, p.4
Evening Advertiser 04.10.1944, p.4 (photo)
See Roll of Honour

**AUBREY
GEORGE THOMAS**
ROYAL ARTILLERY
- Gunner
- Award: Military Medal
- Citation 'for action at Imphal, India'
- Attended Blunsdon School

Source: *North Wilts Herald* 28.07.1944, p.5
Evening Advertiser 26.07.1944, p.2 (photo)
Evening Advertiser 23.09.1944, p.3 (photo)

AXFORD
T. L.
ROYAL ENGINEERS
- Staff Sergeant
- Award: British Empire Medal (Military Division)

Source: *Great Western Railway Magazine* March 1946, p.62

BAILEY
T. H.
ROYAL NAVY
- Able Seaman
- Award: British Empire Medal

Source: *Evening Advertiser* 30.09.1942, p.4 (photo)

BARRATT
F. W. G.
- Major
- Award: OBE (Military Division)

Source: Swindon Council Minutes 24.04.45, p.183

BARRETT
DENNIS HUGH BRYAN
ROYAL NAVY
- Lieutenant Commander
- Award: Distinguished Service Cross

Source: *Evening Advertiser* 02.08.2010, p.22
Evening Advertiser 08.08.1940, p.4
Evening Advertiser 16.05.1945, p.2 (photo)
Evening Advertiser 19.06.1945, p.5 (photo)
Evening Advertiser 18.09.1945, p.2
Wroughton History Group – Book 7 (1997), p.8
Wroughton History Group - Book - 8 (2002), p.8
Wroughton History Group – Book 9 (2009), p.42-3,
Wroughton History Group - Book 10 (2016), p.147
See Prisoners of War

BEALE
COLIN LESLIE
ROYAL ARTILLERY
- Gunner
- Award: British Empire Medal
- Helped air crew escape from crashed plane which was laden with incendiary bombs, at a RAF station

Source: *North Wilts Herald* 17.07.1942, p.4
North Wilts Herald 22.04.1943, p.4 (photo)
Great Western Railway Magazine September 1942, p.163,
Evening Advertiser 14.07.1942, p.1
Evening Advertiser 16.04.1943, p.1 (photo)

BEAVES
H. H.
WILTSHIRE REGIMENT/
ROYAL ARMY ORDNANCE
CORPS
- Award: Mentioned in Despatches

Source: *Evening Advertiser* 05.08.1945, p.2

BESWICK
ROBERT EASTCOTT
EDWARD
- Lieutenant
- Award: MBE, Mentioned in Despatches and Bar
- *Evening Advertiser* gives him rank of Lieutenant Commander

Source: *North Wilts Herald* 06.04.1945, p.3 (photo)
Evening Advertiser 16.05.1945, p.2 (photo)

BICKFORD
EDWARD OSCAR
ROYAL NAVY (submarine Salmon)
- Commander
- Award: Distinguished Service Order
- Killed when submarine was sunk

Source: *North Wilts Herald* 14.07.1940, p5
Evening Advertiser 22.07.1940, p.1 (photo)
See Roll of Honour

BLACKWELL
RONALD GORDON
ROYAL AIR FORCE Voluntary Reserve
- Sergeant Air Gunner
- Award: Distinguished Flying Medal
- Attended Gorse Hill School, Swindon

Source: *North Wilts Herald* 11.08.1944, p.5
North Wilts Herald 28.07.1944, p.8 (photo)
Evening Advertiser 22.07.1944 pp. 3/5 (photo)
Evening Advertiser 05.08.1944, p.4

BLYTHE
ALEXANDER CONWAY
ROYAL AIR FORCE Voluntary Reserve
- Flight Lieutenant
- Award: Distinguished Flying Cross

Source: *North Wilts Herald* 05.01.1945, p.2
Evening Advertiser 30.12.1944, p.5

BRADY
HENRY GEORGE
ROYAL AIR FORCE Voluntary Reserve
- Sergeant
- Award: Distinguished Flying Medal

Source: *North Wilts Herald* 26.05.1944, p.8
Evening Advertiser 19.05.1944, p.5

BRAIN
JACK
ROYAL AIR FORCE
- Squadron Leader
- Award: Air Flying Cross and Mentioned in Despatches
- AFC for "Outstanding leadership and devotion to duty"
- MiD for "bravery whilst carrying out a bombing raid in Stavangar"

Source: *North Wilts Herald* 16.06.1944, p.4 (photo)
Evening Advertiser 14.06.1944, p.2

BRADDICK
J. R.
ROYAL ARTILLERY
- Major
- Award: Military Cross
- Mrs Braddick was a director of Reynolds & Co, boot factors of Swindon

Source: *Evening Advertiser* 05.02.1943, p.4 (photo)

BREWER
JOHN ARTHUR
- Major
- Award: Mentioned in Despatches

Source: *North Wilts Herald* 03.09.1943, p.8 (photo)
North Wilts Herald 11.02.1944, p.5 (photo)
Evening Advertiser 27.08.1943, p.4 (photo)
Evening Advertiser 04.09.1943, p.3
Evening Advertiser 04.02.1944, p.1 (photo)
See Prisoners of War

BUTLER
ALFRED HENRY
ROYAL ARMY SERVICE CORPS
- Award: British Empire Medal (Military Division)

Source: *North Wilts Herald* 29.03.1945, p.2

BYE
JOHN PERCIVAL
ROYAL NAVY
- Chief Yeoman of Signals
- Award: Distinguished Service Medal and Mentioned in Despatches
- Awarded for work at Anzio

Source: *North Wilts Herald* 04.08.1944, p.4
North Wilts Herald 11.08.1944, p.8 (photo)
Evening Advertiser 04.08.1944, p.4 (photo)

CARTER
ALBERT HORACE
ROYAL NAVY
- Able Seaman
- Award: Distinguished Service Medal

Source: *Evening Advertiser* 04.02.1943, p.2 (photo)

GALLANTRY AWARDS AND MEDALS

CARTER
ALBERT LESLIE
ROYAL AIR FORCE
- Squadron Leader (Royal Navy)
- Award: Distinguished Flying Cross; Mentioned in Despatches
- Attended Commonweal School, Swindon

Source: Wroughton War Memorial
North Wilts Herald 06.04.1945, p.5
Evening Advertiser 02.04.1945, p.5
Evening Advertiser 09.04.1945, p.2
Evening Advertiser 05.10.1945, p.4
Wroughton History Group - Book 10 (2016), pp.75 & 102
See Roll of Honour

CLARK-KENNEDY
A.J.
LANCERS
- Lieutenant
- Award: Military Cross
- Son of Mrs Clark Kennedy of Hannington Wick
- Rev Clark-Kennedy (deceased), ex vicar of Highworth

Source: *North Wilts Herald* 21.06.1940

CLINTON
GILBERT JAMES
MERCHANT NAVY (SS Tucurinca)
- Third Engineer Officer
- Award: MBE

Source: CWGC
See Roll of Honour

COLE
WILLIAM GEOFFREY
ROYAL AIR FORCE Voluntary Reserve
- Flight Lieutenant
- Award: Distinguished Flying Cross

Source: *North Wilts Herald* 17.09.1943, p.5 (photo)
Evening Advertiser 10.09.1943, p.4

COOLE
SIDNEY GEORGE
ROYAL AIR FORCE Voluntary Reserve
- Flight Sergeant
- Award: Distinguished Flying Medal
- For "Gallantry displayed in flying operations against the enemy"
- Attended Ferndale Road School, Swindon

Source: *North Wilts Herald* 07.07.1944, p.8 (photo)
Evening Advertiser 03.07.1944, p.4 (photo)

COX
JESSE EDWIN
ROYAL CANADIAN AIR FORCE
- Warrant Officer
- Award: Distinguished Flying Cross

Source: *North Wilts Herald* 30.10.1942, p.5

CUBBAGE
BRIAN STANLEY
ROYAL AIR FORCE Voluntary Reserve
- Pilot Officer (Air Gunner)
- Award: Distinguished Flying Medal
- Died: 15.02.1944
- Attended Pinehurst School, Swindon

Source: *North Wilts Herald* 26.05.1944, p.5 (photo)
North Wilts Herald 12.12.1944, p.8
Evening Advertiser 11.12.1944, p.5
Evening Advertiser 22.05.1944, p.1 (photo)
See Roll of Honour

DAVIES
KENNETH ALBERT WILLIAM
- Lance Corporal
- Award: Mentioned in Despatches
- Attended Sanford Street School, Swindon

Source: *Evening Advertiser* 19.02.1942, p.1 (photo)

DAW
R. G.
ROYAL AIR FORCE
- Flight Sergeant
- Award: Mentioned in Despatches: African Star
- Attended Even Swindon School, Swindon

Source: *Evening Advertiser* 13.04.1943, p.8
Evening Advertiser 24.01.1944, p.2 (photo)

DAY
SIDNEY FRANK
ROYAL NAVY (HMS Wyvern)
- Petty Officer Stoker
- Award: British Empire Medal: Mentioned in Despatches
- Died 22.02.1943

Source: St Augustine Church Memorial
North Wilts Herald 05.03.1943, p.5 (photo)
North Wilts Herald 09.07.1943, p.8 (photo)
Evening Advertiser 27.02.1943, p.5 (photo)
Evening Advertiser 07.07.1943, p.4 (photo) lists citation for Mention in Despatches
See Roll of Honour

DUNFORD
REGINALD JAMES
ROYAL NAVY
Chief Engineroom Artificer
- Award: Distinguished Service Medal; Distinguished Service Cross; Africa Star
- Distinguished Service Medal for gallantry while on convoy work
- Distinguished Service Cross for 'skilful engineering ... bringing back a ship after ramming and sinking a U boat'
- Attended Euclid Street School, Swindon

Source: *North Wilts Herald* 27.02.1942, p.4
North Wilts Herald 29.01.1943, p.5 (photo)
North Wilts Herald 25.02.1944, p.5 (photo)
Evening Advertiser 12.02.1942, p.1 (photo)
Evening Advertiser 26.02.1942, p.1
Evening Advertiser 11.07.1942, p.1
Evening Advertiser 23.01.1943, p.4

DURNELL
CLARENCE W.
ROYAL NAVY
- S/M Engineroom Artificer
- Award: British Empire Medal
- For bravery in action off the coast of Norway
- Attended Sanford Street School, Swindon

Source: *North Wilts Herald* 27.02.1942, p.4 (photo)
www.highworthhistoricalsociety.co.uk

DURNFORD
CYRIL
ROYAL ENGINEERS
- Signalman
- Award: Africa Star

Source: *Evening Advertiser* 25.02.1944, p.2

EAGLE
JOHN WILLIAM
ROYAL CORPS OF SIGNALS
- Major (temp)
- Award: MBE

Source: *Evening Advertiser* 30.06.1945, p.3

EASLEY
JOHN
ROYAL NAVY
- Chief Engineroom Artificer
- Award: Mentioned in Despatches

Source: *Evening Advertiser* 19.02.1943, p.1

ELWELL
PAUL BINGHAM
ROYAL AIR FORCE
- Squadron Leader
- Award: Distinguished Flying Cross
- Sale of his medals in *Evening Advertiser* 1.10.2013, p.15

Source: *North Wilts Herald* 21.07.1944, p.4 (photo)
Evening Advertiser 19.07.1944, pp. 3/5 (photo)

GALLANTRY AWARDS AND MEDALS

FARRIER
ERNEST CHARLES
ROYAL NAVY (HMS Niger)
- Petty Officer Stoker
- Award: Mentioned in Despatches
- Died 06.07.1943

Source: CWGC
See Roll of Honour

FELL
ROBERT LONSDALE
ROYAL AIR FORCE Voluntary Reserve
- Flight Lieutenant
- Award: Distinguished Flying Cross
- Attended Radley and Sandhurst Schools

Source: *North Wilts Herald* 18.08.1944, p.3 (photo)
Evening Advertiser 23.09.1944, p.2 (photo)

FELTHAM
EDGAR THOMAS
ROYAL AIR FORCE
- Sergeant Wireless Operator/Air Gunner
- Award: Distinguished Flying Medal

Source: *North Wilts Herald* 12.09.1941, p.4 (photo)

FISHER
CHARLES E. P.
RECONNAISSANCE CORPS
- Sergeant
- Award: Military Medal
- Medal won in Sicily

Source: *Great Western Railway Magazine* April 1944, p.65 & May 1945, p.83
North Wilts Herald 09.03.1945, p.5
North Wilts Herald 18.05.1945, p.5 (photo)
Evening Advertiser 15.05.1945, p.4 (photo)

FISHER
JACK
- Sergeant
- Award: Military Medal

Source: *North Wilts Herald* 29.10.1943, p.4 (photo)
Evening Advertiser 25.10.1943, p.8 (photo)

FORTUNE
S. H.
ROYAL AIR FORCE
- Flight Sergeant
- Award: Distinguished Flying Medal

Source: *Great Western Railway Magazine* February 1946, p.42

FRANKIS
W. E.
HOME GUARD
- Award: British Empire Medal

Source: *Great Western Railway Magazine* August 1944, p.118

GALLANTRY AWARDS AND MEDALS

FULLER
FRED
ROYAL AIR FORCE
- Flight Lieutenant
- Award: Certificate of Good Service

Source: *North Wilts Herald* 12.04.1946, p.3

GILLIGAN
FREDERICK JOHN
ROYAL INNISKILLING FUSILIERS
- Sergeant
- Award: Military Medal
- Died 01.10.1945

Source: *Evening Advertiser* 10.11.1945, p.6
See Roll of Honour

GOODRIDGE
CHARLES HENRY
ROYAL AIR FORCE
- Flight Sergeant
- Award: British Empire Medal; Mentioned in Despatches

Source: *North Wilts Herald* 16.02.1945, p.3
Evening Advertiser 17.09.1943, p.1
The Euclidean Christmas 1943, p.3

GREEN
JOHN
ROYAL TANK REGIMENT
- Lance Corporal
- Award: Military Medal
- Attended Sanford Street School

Source: *North Wilts Herald* 22.06.1945, p.5
Evening Advertiser 16.06.1945, p.1
Evening Advertiser 20.06.1945, p.2 (photo)

GUNN
LESLIE GEORGE
ROYAL ARTILLERY
- Lance Bombardier
- Award: Military Medal

Source: *North Wilts Herald* 07.08.1945, p.5 (photo)
Evening Advertiser 10.08.1945, p.2 (photo)

HALL
DAVID MILDMAY MORDAUNT
ROYAL BERKSHIRE REGIMENT
- Major
- Award: Military Cross
- His "fearlessness and determination was an inspiration to his men and was worth of the highest praise"

Source: *North Wilts Herald* 24.08.1945, p.6

HAINES
C. V.
ROYAL AIR FORCE
- Flight Lieutenant
- Award: Air Flying Cross
- Brother of **W.J. HAINES** see below

Evening Advertiser 26.01.1944, p.1 (photo)

GALLANTRY AWARDS AND MEDALS

**HAINES
W. J.**
ROYAL NAVY
- Chief Petty Officer
- Award: British Empire Medal
- Brother of **C.V. HAINES** see above

Source: *Evening Advertiser* 26.01.1944, p.1 (photo)

**HALLIDAY
WILLIAM C. C.**
ROYAL ARTILLERY
- Gunner
- Award: Order of the British Empire
- "For meritorious service in action"
- Attended Gorse Hill School, Swindon

Source: *North Wilts Herald* 06.03.1942, p.4
North Wilts Herald 10.04.1942, p.6 (photo)
Evening Advertiser 12.01.1942, p.1 (photo)
Evening Advertiser 02.04.1942, p.1 (photo)

**HAYNES
W. B.**
ROYAL AIR FORCE
- Corporal
- Award: Mentioned in Despatches

Source: *Evening Advertiser* 30.06.1945, p.2

**HAYWARD
LESLIE JOSEPH**
ROYAL NAVY
- Chief Engineroom Artificer
- Award: Distinguished Service Medal
- "For gallantry, tenacity and devotion to duty in patrols in the Aegean"
- Attended Euclid Street School, Swindon

Source: *The Euclidean* Christmas 1945, p.3
North Wilts Herald 29.06.45, p.5 (photo)
Evening Advertiser 26.06.1945, p.2 (photo)

**HEAMES
IAN LEWIS CHARLES**
ROYAL AIR FORCE
- Flying Officer
- Award: Distinguished Flying Cross
- Attended Jennings Street School, Swindon

Source: *Great Western Railway Magazine* September 1945, p.148
Evening Advertiser 25.05.1945, p.1

GALLANTRY AWARDS AND MEDALS

HEAVENS
ROBERT ERIC
SPECIAL AIR SERVICE
REGIMENT
- Sergeant
- Award: Mentioned in Despatches
- Captured and shot 07.07.1944
- Attended Clarence Street School, Swindon

Source: *Great Western Railway Magazine* October 1944 p.160
Great Western Railway Magazine August 1945, p.133
North Wilts Herald 06.07.1945, p.5 (photo)
Evening Advertiser 15.08.1944, p.5 (photo)
Evening Advertiser 29.06.1945, p.2 (photo)
See Roll of Honour

HILL
HAROLD
ROYAL ENGINEERS
- Major
- Award: Mentioned in Despatches

Source: *North Wilts Herald* 20.04.1945, p.4

HOLLOWAY
REGINALD L.
ROYAL NAVY
- Supply Assistant
- Award: Distinguished Service Medal
- "For gallantry, skill and resolution in a brilliant night action south of Taranto.. in which without hurt or loss to the Royal Navy, 10 enemy supply ships were wholly destroyed"

Source: *North Wilts Herald* 05.05.1942, p.4 (photo)
Evening Advertiser 10.03.1942, p.1

HORNBLOW
F. H.
ROYAL NAVY
- Chief Electrical Artificer
- Award: Distinguished Service Medal
- "For conspicuous service while taking part in the action against the German ship Scharnhorst"
- Attended Clarence Street School, Swindon

Source: *North Wilts Herald* 24.03.1944, p.3 (photo)
Evening Advertiser 22.03.1944, p.5 (photo)

HOUNSELL
S.
ROYAL AIR FORCE
- Corporal
- Award: Mentioned in Despatches

Source: *Great Western Railway Magazine* November 1946, p.254

HUNNEX
A. W.
LONDON IRISH RIFLES
- Corporal
- Award: British Empire Medal

Source: *North Wilts Herald* 16.06.1944, p.4 (photo)
Evening Advertiser 16.06.1944, p.2 (photo)

JACKSON
G. W. H.
ROYAL ELECTRICAL AND MECHANICAL ENGINEERS
- Warrant Officer
- Award: Croix de Guerre
- For gallantry on the Normandy beaches

Source: *Evening Advertiser* 01.08.1945, p.2

JONES
E. A.
- Award: Military Cross
- For gallantry at Anzio

Source: *North Wilts Herald* 09.06.1944, p.8 (photo)

JOSLING
JOHN BASIL
ROYAL AIR FORCE Voluntary Reserve
- Flying Officer Pilot
- Award: Distinguished Flying Cross
- Died: 24.07.1944
- Husband of Patricia Josling of Lydiard Millicent

Source: CWGC
See Roll of Honour

KEITH-ROACH
MARTIN
ROYAL NAVY
- Lieutenant
- Award: Distinguished Service Cross

Source: *North Wilts Herald* 05.08.1940, p2

KEYLOCK
WILLIAM HENRY
ROYAL NAVY
- Telegraphist
- Award: Mentioned in Despatches and 2 Bars
- Died 18.02.1944

Source: *North Wilts Herald* 31.03.1944, p.5
North Wilts Herald 06.04.1944, p.4
North Wilts Herald 29.03.1945, p.6 (photo)
See Roll of Honour

KING
ERNEST WILLIAM
ROYAL NAVY
- Chief Petty Officer
- Award: British Empire Medal

Source: *North Wilts Herald* 22.01.1943, p.5 (photo)

KNIGHTS
D. R.
ROYAL ENGINEERS
- Major
- Award: MBE (Military Division)

Source: *Great Western Railway Magazine* February 1946, p.42

LAING
DONALD
ROYAL AIR FORCE
- Flight Lieutenant
- Award: Mentioned in Despatches & 2 bars
- Died 03.09.1942

Source: CWGC
See Roll of Honour

LANG/LANGWORTHY
JOHN
ROYAL TANK REGIMENT
- Sergeant/Instructor
- Award: Military Medal
- *Evening Advertiser* lists him as Langworthy

Source: *North Wilts Herald* 09.10.1942, p.5 (photo)
Evening Advertiser 2.10.1942, p.8 (photo)

LLOYD
WILLIAM
ROYAL ARMOURED CORPS
- Squadron Sergeant Major
- Award: Distinguished Conduct Medal
- "In recognition of gallant and distinguished service in the Middle East"

Source: *North Wilts Herald* 30.10.1942, p.5 (photo)
Evening Advertiser 16.10.1942, p.4
Evening Advertiser 24.10.1942, p.2 (photo)

LONG
CECIL REGINALD
ROYAL AIR FORCE
- Sergeant
- Award: Distinguished Service Medal
- Attended Gorse Hill School, Swindon

Source: *North Wilts Herald* 01.01.1943, p.4
Evening Advertiser 29.12.1942, p.6 (photo)

LORD
DAVID SAMUEL
ROYAL AIR FORCE
- Flight Lieutenant
- Award: Distinguished Flying Cross

Source: *Evening Advertiser* 22.01.1945, p.3
Evening Advertiser 16.07.1943, p.4

McCANDLISH
ALEX
ROYAL AIR FORCE
- Flight Lieutenant
- Award: Distinguished Flying Cross
- His father Dr McCandlish was on the staff of the GWR Medical Fund Society for 20 years, before moving to Luton
- Attended Swindon Secondary School

Source: *North Wilts Herald* 04.06.1943, p.4

McCARTHY
ROBERT W.
ROYAL AIR FORCE
- Leading aircraftman
- Award: Distinguished Flying Medal
- For gallantry during a bombing raid
- Attended Commonweal School
- Died 06.12.1942

Source: *Evening Advertiser* 21.06.2010, p.16
North Wilts Herald 28.06.1940, p.3
Evening Advertiser 25.06.1940, p.3
The Euclidean Summer 1943
The Euclidean Christmas 1943
Headlandian Summer 1946, p.30
See Roll of Honour

MATTHEWS
DOUGLAS SPENCER
ROYAL AIR FORCE
- Pilot Officer
- Award: Distinguished Flying Medal
- Brother of **GORDON MATTHEWS**, see Prisoners of War

Source: Swindonian Autumn 1941, p.886
Evening Advertiser 14.1.1942
Evening Advertiser 15.1.1942
Evening Advertiser 18.05.1945, p.2
North Wilts Herald 16.01.1942, p.3 (photo)
See Roll of Honour

MATTICK
STANLEY RICHARD
ROYAL AIR FORCE Voluntary Reserve
- Flight Sergeant
- Award: Distinguished Flying Medal
- For "Gallantry and devotion to duty in execution of air operations", "Displaying great vigilance he has been able to direct his pilot skilfully to evade enemy fighters and defences"
- Died 02.01.1944

Source: *North Wilts Herald* 22.10.1943, p.6 (photo)
North Wilts Herald 29.03.1945, p.6 (photo)
North Wilts Herald 16.03.1945, p.5 (photo);
Evening Advertiser 18.10.1943, p.8 (photo)
Evening Advertiser 07.01.1944, p.1
Evening Advertiser 15.01.1944, p.3
Stratton Green Baptist Church Memorial
See Roll of Honour

MEAD
LES
17/21 LANCERS
- Sergeant
- Award: Military Medal

Source: *Wroughton History Group - Book 9* (2009), p.103

MEECH
H. E.
ROYAL ARMY SERVICE CORPS
- Staff Quartermaster Sergeant
- Award: Mentioned in Despatches
- Attended Jennings Street School, Swindon

Source: *North Wilts Herald* 17.08.1945, p.4 (photo)

MONEY
LEONARD
HAMPSHIRE REGIMENT
- Lance Corporal
- Award: Military Medal

Source: *Evening Advertiser* 11.05.1945, p.8

MILLS
TONY
ROYAL AIR FORCE REGIMENT
- Flying Officer
- Award: Mentioned in Despatches

Source: *North Wilts Herald* 13.08.1943, p.4 (photo)

MOORE
TOM HENRY
- Award: Military Medal
- Discharged from the Army as a result of losing a leg in a train accident

Source: *North Wilts Herald* 16.07.1943, p.5

MOULDEN
NORMAN CHARLES
FLEET AIR ARM
- Leading aircraftman
- Award: Mentioned in Despatches
- Attended Westcott Place School, Swindon
- Died 01.11.1941

Source: *North Wilts Herald* 14.11.1941, p.5
Evening Advertiser 06.11.1941, p.4
Evening Advertiser 07.11.1941, p.3
See Roll of Honour

MULLARD
J. H.
ROYAL CORPS OF SIGNALS
- Signaller
- Award: Military Medal
- Delivered a message under heavy artillery fire while wounded in arm and thigh

Source: *Evening Advertiser* 04.11.1941 (photo)

NEW
V. H.
ROYAL AIR FORCE
- Sergeant
- Award: Distinguished Flying Medal

Source: Swindonian p.923

NEWMAN
PHILLIP HENRY
KINGS ROYAL RIFLE CORPS
- Sergeant
- Award: Military Medal

Source: *North Wilts Herald* 24.08.1945, p.5

NORRIS
EDMUND RICHARD
WILTSHIRE REGIMENT
- Acting Major
- Award: Military Cross

Source: *North Wilts Herald*
09.03.1945, p.5

NOWELL
H. E.
ROYAL AIR FORCE
- Group Captain
- Award: OBE (Military Division)
- Attended King William Street School, Swindon

Source: *Evening Advertiser*
27.05.1943
Swindonian p.923

NUTBEEM
CLAUDE
- Captain
- Award: Mentioned in Despatches
- For "Gallant and distinguished service in North Africa"
- Attended Sanford Street School, Swindon

Source: *North Wilts Herald*
05.11.1943, p.5 (photo)
Evening Advertiser 01.11.1943, p.4 (photo)

OSMAN
WALTER EDWARD
ROYAL SUSSEX REGIMENT
- Sergeant
- Award: Military Medal
- Attended Wroughton School

Source: *North Wilts Herald*
28.07.1944, p.4
Wroughton History Group - Book 9 (2009), p.101
Wroughton History Group - Book 10 (2016), p.110
Evening Advertiser 22.05.1944, p.2 (photo)
Evening Advertiser 10.10.1944, p.5

PEART
ALBERT
ROYAL AIR FORCE
- Flying Officer
- Award: Mentioned in Despatches
- Attended Commonweal School

Source: *North Wilts Herald*
13.02.1943, p.4 (photo)
Evening Advertiser 12.02.1943, p.1 (photo), p.2

PEBWORTH
DENNIS ARTHUR
ROYAL AIR FORCE Voluntary Reserve
- Flight Lieutenant (Observer)
- Award: Distinguished Flying Cross
- Died 24.08.1942

Source:
North Wilts Herald 28.08.1942, p.8 (photo)
North Wilts Herald 04.09.1942, p.3
North Wilts Herald 30.10.1942, p.5 (photo)
Evening Advertiser 29.08.1942, p.3 (photo)
Evening Advertiser 28.10.1942, p.4 (photo)
Evening Advertiser 04.03.1943, p.1 (photo)
Wills Works Magazine, August 1945, p.14
See Roll of Honour

PHILLIPS
R. L.
ROYAL AIR FORCE
- Group Captain
- Award: Mentioned in Despatches and Bar

Source: *Evening Advertiser* 07.09.1943, p.6

PONT
ARTHUR STANLEY
ROYAL ARTILLLERY
- Captain
- Award: Military Medal; Order of the British Empire

Source: *Evening Advertiser* 23.06.1945, p.4

PRINCE
WILLIAM ALBERT RYAN
ROYAL EAST KENT REGIMENT
- Corporal
- Award: Military Medal; Africa Star
- Attended Holy Rood School, Swindon

Source: *Evening Advertiser* 27.10.1944, p.8
North Wilts Herald 15.09.1944, p.8 (photo)

QUARRELL
WILLIAM HAROLD
ROYAL NAVY (HM Submarine Tigris)
Petty Officer
- Award: Distinguished Service Medal
- *Evening Advertiser* says he had the Distinguished Service Order
- Died 10.03.1943

North Wilts Herald 03.03.1944, p.8 (photo)
Evening Advertiser 18.11.1943, p.2
Evening Advertiser 2.03.1944, p.4 (photo)
See Roll of Honour

RAWLINGS
RONALD VICTOR
ROYAL NAVY
- Petty Officer
- Award: Mentioned in Despatches

Source: *Evening Advertiser* 20.09.1944, p.4

REYNOLDS
BERNARD ALLEN
ROYAL AIR FORCE
- Sergeant Pilot
- Award: Distinguished Flying Medal
- Attended Commonweal School, Swindon
- Died 08.08.1944

Source: *The Euclidean* Summer 1943, p.5
North Wilts Herald 25.06.1943, p.5 (photo)
North Wilts Herald 03.12.1943, p.3 (photo)
North Wilts Herald 18.08.1944, p.5 (photo)
Evening Advertiser 19.06.1943, p.1 (photo
Evening Advertiser 01.12.1943, p.8 (photo)
Evening Advertiser 11.08.1944, p.8 (photo)
Swindonian Summer 1945, p.6
See Roll of Honour

ROUND
FRANK DESMOND
ROYAL AIR FORCE 35 Squadron
- Flight Lieutenant
- Award: Distinguished Flying Medal
- Died: 05.07.1944
- Husband of Frances Round of Highworth

Source: CWGC
See Roll of Honour

RYAN
RICHARD JOHN
HAMMERSLEY
ROYAL NAVY (HMS President)
- Lieutenant Commander
- Award: George Cross
- Husband of Margaret Ryan, of Wroughton
- George Cross Citation on CWGC
- Died 21.09.1940 while defusing a bomb in Dagenham, Essex

Source: CWGC
London Gazette 17.12.1940
See Roll of Honour

ROSE
CLIFFORD H.
- Lieutenant Colonel
- Mentioned in Despatches

Evening Advertiser 30.11.1943, p.4

SCOTT
JOHN
BORDER REGIMENT
- Despatch Rider
- Award: George Medal

Source: *North Wilts Herald* 01.05.1942, p.4 (photo)
North Wilts Herald 24.04.1942, p.3

SELBY
FRANK GORDON
ROYAL NAVY
- Petty Officer
- Award: Distinguished Service Medal; Mentioned in Despatches
- DSO for "skill and enterprise in successful patrols".
- Mentioned in Despatches for returning "to sinking ship to provide sailors with lifesaving apparatus"
- Attended Swindon Secondary School

Source: *Evening Advertiser* 01.09.1941, p.3
Evening Advertiser 03.09.1941, p.2 (photo)
Evening Advertiser 25.08.1942, p.4 (photo)
Evening Advertiser 04.05.1943, p.4 (photo)
North Wilts Herald 05.09.1941, p.4 (photo)
North Wilts Herald 12.12.1941, p.4
North Wilts Herald 07.05.1943, p.5
Swindonian p.923

SHARP
SIDNEY
ROYAL AIR FORCE
- Acting Squadron Leader
- Award: Distinguished Flying Cross
- "For skill and devotion to duty on two tours of operations"
- Attended Euclid Street School, Swindon

Source: *The Euclidean* Christmas 1945, p.3

SHEPPARD
STUART
- Lance Corporal
- Award: Military Medal
- Attended Headlands School

Source: *Headlandian* Summer 1945, p.22
Headlandian Summer 1946, p.30

SMITH
JOSEPH GEORGE
WILTSHIRE REGIMENT
- Company Sergeant Major
- Award: Military Medal and Bar
- Died 16.02.1945

Source: *North Wilts Herald* 27.10.1944, p.5
North Wilts Herald 27.10.1944, p.5
North Wilts Herald 02.03.1945, p.4 (photo)
Evening Advertiser 09.09.1944, p.8 (photo)
Evening Advertiser 21.10.1944, p.5
Evening Advertiser 25.05.1945, p.1
Stanton Fitzwarren War Memorial
See Roll of Honour

STAFFORD
HAROLD A.
ROYAL ENGINEERS
- Major
- Award: OBE
- "In recognition of his services as Assistant Superintendent of Air Ministry at Valetta, Malta"
- Son of J Stafford, Headmaster of Clarence Street School, Swindon

Source: *Evening Advertiser* 01.06.1943, p.2 (photo)

GALLANTRY AWARDS AND MEDALS

STARR
NORMAN JOHN
ROYAL AIR FORCE
- Wing Commander (Pilot)
- Award: Distinguished Flying Cross and Bar
- Died 08.01.1945
- Attended Cotham School Bristol

Source: *North Wilts Herald* 16.04.1943, p.5
North Wilts Herald 15.06.1945, p.5
Evening Advertiser 09.04.1943, p.5
Evening Advertiser 09.06.1945, p.2
Swindon Heritage magazine, special edition September 2015
Memorial in Radnor Street Cemetery, Swindon
See Roll of Honour

STEPHENS
IAN RADNOR
ROYAL AIR FORCE
- Acting Squadron Leader
- Award: Distinguished Flying Cross and Bar

Source: *North Wilts Herald* 21.05.1943, p.5

STEWART (STUART)
NORMAN
ROYAL NAVY
- Able Seaman
- Award: Distinguished Service Medal
- Nominated for a Victoria Cross for "saving the life of a wounded officer during the first battle of Narvik"

Source: *Evening Advertiser* 17.05.1940, p.1
Evening Advertiser 17.05.2010, p.16
London Gazette 05.07.1940, p.4152

STRANGE
DENNIS JAMES
ROYAL AIR FORCE
- Pilot Officer
- Award: MBE

Source: *North Wilts Herald* 21.01.1944, p.5 (photo)
Evening Advertiser 17.09.1943, p.1
Evening Advertiser 18.01.1944, p.2 (photo)

STRANGE
JAMES
ROYAL AIR FORCE
- Flight Sergeant
- Award: Mentioned in Despatches
- Attended The College, Victoria Road, Swindon

Source: *North Wilts Herald* 26.03.1943, p.3 (photo)

STROUD
H. V.
ROYAL NAVY
- Acting Chief Engineroom Artificer
- Award: Mentioned in Despatches

Source: *Great Western Railway Magazine* October 1945, p163

STURMEY
K. N.
1st SPECIAL AIR SERVICE
- Parachutist Sergeant
- Award: Mentioned in Despatches

Source: *Great Western Railway Magazine* November 1945, p.182
www.rodbournehistory.org

SUMMERS
STANLEY GORDON
ROYAL NAVY (HMS Vivacious)
- Petty Officer
- Award: Mentioned in Despatches
- For "Distinguished service in the Navy"

Source: *North Wilts Herald* 21.08.1942, p.5 (photo)
Evening Advertiser 15.08.1942, p.4 (photo)

TANNER
ALFRED
16th PUNJAB REGIMENT
- Lieutenant
- Award: Certificate of Gallantry
- For distinguished service in Burma

Source: *Evening Advertiser* 02.10.1944, p.5

TANNER
W. S.
ROYAL ENGINEERS
- Sergeant
- Award: British Empire Medal (Military Division)

Source: *Great Western Railway Magazine* September 1946, p.206

THOMAS
JOHN EDWIN
ROYAL AIR FORCE
- Warrant Officer
- Award: Distinguished Flying Cross

Source: *Evening Advertiser* 11.11.1943, p.3

THOMAS
RHYS HENRY
ROYAL AIR FORCE
- Squadron Leader
- Award: Distinguished Flying Cross & Distinguished Service Order
- DSO for 'magnificent work' in the Dieppe raid 1942
- Attended Commonweal School, Swindon

Source: *The Euclidean* Summer 1942, p.3
Summer 1943, p.4
North Wilts Herald 18.09.1942, p.5
North Wilts Herald 04.09.1942, p.5 (photo)
Evening Advertiser 22.05.1942, p.1
Evening Advertiser 01.09.1942, p.1
Evening Advertiser 11.09.1942, p.3 (photo)

TITCOMB
ERNEST ARTHUR ROBERT
ROYAL NAVY (HMS Searcher)
- Petty Officer
- Award: Distinguished Service Medal
- For "bravery and dauntless resolution when an important convoy was fighting to Malta in face of relentless attacks by day and night"
- Died 22.01.1945

Source: Wroughton War Memorial
www.roll-of-honour.com/wiltshire/wroughton
Evening Advertiser 27.11.1942, p.1 (photo)
Wroughton History Group - Book 10 (2016), pp.79 & 102
See Roll of Honour

**TOMKINS
E. C. C.**
ROYAL AIR FORCE
- Acting Squadron Leader
- Award: Distinguished Flying Cross

Source: *North Wilts Herald* 02.04.1942, p.5 (photo)

**TULL
DESMOND TREVOR**
ROYAL AIR FORCE Voluntary Reserve
- Flying Officer
- Award: Distinguished Flying Cross

Source: *North Wilts Herald* 03.11.1944, p.2
North Wilts Herald 18.12.1944, p.3
Evening Advertiser 01.11.1944, p.4

**VINES
WILLIAM CHARLES HENRY (HARRY)**
ROYAL AIR FORCE Voluntary Reserve
- Flight Sergeant
- Award: Distinguished Flying Medal

Source: *North Wilts Herald* 29.03.1945, p.2
Headlandian Summer 1945, p.22
Swindon Town Council Minutes 19.04.1945, p.175

**WALKER
LESLIE NORMAN**
ROYAL NAVY
- Able Seaman
- Award: Distinguished Service Medal
- Attended Clarence Street School, Swindon
- Died 20.07.1944

Source: *Great Western Railway Magazine* November 1944, p.175
Great Western Railway Magazine November 1945, p.182
North Wilts Herald 03.08.1945, p.8 (photo)
Evening Advertiser 09.08.1944, p.2 (photo)
Evening Advertiser 31.07.1945, p.2
See Roll of Honour

**WARFIELD
ALBERT**
ROYAL AIR FORCE
- Squadron Leader
- Award: Distinguished Flying Cross

Source: *Evening Advertiser* 27.05.1942, p.1

WATKINS
WILLIAM JOHN
ROYAL ARTILLERY
- Bombardier
- Award: George Medal
- For heroism in saving a colleague when troopship was struck by torpedo

Source: *North Wilts Herald* 31.1.1941, p.8 (photo)
North Wilts Herald 14.02.1941, p.3
North Wilts Herald 17.07.1942, p.4 (photo)
Evening Advertiser. 12.02.1941, p.4 (photo)
Evening Advertiser 22.07.1942, p.1 (photo)

WEBB
CHARLES
ROYAL ENGINEERS
- Corporal
- Award: Military Medal
- Attended Sanford Street School, Swindon

Source: *North Wilts Herald* 15.01.1943, p.3
Evening Advertiser 12.01.1943, p.4 (photo)

WEBB-MORRIS
TED
ROYAL TANK REGIMENT
- Regimental Sergeant Major
- Award: Military Medal
- Attended Lethbridge Road School, Swindon

Source: *North Wilts Herald* 04.09.1942, p4 (photo)
North Wilts Herald 12.05.1944, p.5 (photo)
Evening Advertiser 28.08.1942, p.1 (photo)
Evening Advertiser 24.12.1943, p.1 (photo)
Evening Advertiser 06.05.1944, p.2 (photo)
See Prisoners of War

WHITEHOUSE
JOHN S.
ROYAL AIR FORCE
- Sergeant Flight Engineer
- Award: Distinguished Flying Medal
- Attended Sanford Street School, Swindon

Source: *Great Western Railway Magazine* February 1945, p.32
North Wilts Herald 16.02.1945, p.8
North Wilts Herald 22.12.1945, p.8 (photo)
Evening Advertiser 16.12.1944, p.2 (photo)

WICKHAM
ANTHONY (TONY) T.
ROYAL AIR FORCE
- Flying Officer
- Award: Distinguished Flying Cross

Source: *North Wilts Herald* 13.02.1943, p.4

**WILMER
KENNETH
ROYAL AIR FORCE**
- Corporal
- Award: Mentioned in Despatches
- Attended High School, Bath Road, Swindon

Source: *North Wilts Herald* 05.05.1944, p.5 (photo)
Evening Advertiser 02.05.1944, p.8 (photo)

**WINTER
A.
PARATROOP REGIMENT**
- Corporal
- Award: Mentioned in Despatches

Source: *Evening Advertiser* 22.09.1944, p.4 (photo)

**YATES
F. W.
ROYAL ARMY ORDNANCE CORPS**
- Major
- Award: Mentioned in Despatches

Source: *Great Western Railway Magazine* December 1946, p.279

www.ingramcontent.com/pod-product-compliance
Lightning Source LLC
LaVergne TN
LVHW021119080426
835510LV00012B/1754